All about
HORSES

THE ANSWERS TO THE QUESTIONS
YOU HAVEN'T THOUGHT ABOUT

Copyright © 2025 by WhyWhatHuh

All rights reserved.

No part of this book may be reproduced, distributed, or transmitted in any form or by any means, including photocopying, recording, or other electronic or mechanical methods, without the prior written permission of the publisher, except in the case of brief quotations embodied in critical reviews and certain other non-commercial uses permitted by copyright law. For permission requests, write to the publisher.

2 Edition

Legal Notice:

While the author has made every effort to ensure the accuracy of the information contained in this book, the information is provided without warranty, express or implied. Neither the author nor the publisher shall be held liable for any damages caused directly or indirectly by the information contained in this book.

A horse, a horse! My kingdom for a horse!

William Shakespeare

CONTENT

Introduction	7
Before Starting	8
The WHATs	9
1. What makes a horse's hoof so tough that it thumps the ground without getting damaged?	10
2. What's the deal with horses sleeping standing up—are they part unicorn?	12
3. What cool tricks do wild horses use to survive out there?	14
4. What's behind a horse's neigh—do they have their own language?	17
5. What's the scoop on where horse coat patterns come from?	19
6. What can horse behavior teach us about how we interact with each other?	21
7. What role did horses have in building ancient societies that we often overlook?	23
8. What's the surprising reason horses get along with other barn animals?	26
9. What do horses' problem-solving skills reveal about their smarts?	28
10. What's the story behind the phrase "don't look a gift horse in the mouth"?	31
11. What does a horse's mane and tail say about its feelings?	33
12. What common horse myths have been busted by science?	35
The WHYs	39
1. Why do horses stick together in herds—are they secretly social?	
	40

2. Why do some horses seem to sense our feelings—what's their secret?   43

3. Why are some horses more unique in personality—does mood matter?   45

4. Why do horses have great memories—can they recall a ride from years ago?   48

5. Why do certain breeds shine in specific sports—what's the reason?   51

6. Why are horses labeled "cold-blooded" or "hot-blooded"—what does it mean?   53

7. Why do horses nuzzle and groom each other—just friendly, or more?   56

8. Why can we tell a horse's age and health by its teeth—are they nature's age detectors?   58

9. Why is horse therapy becoming a go-to for helping people?   60

10. Why do horses kick—what's behind this instinct?   63

11. Why do some horses bond more closely with humans than with each other?   65

12. Why is a horse's sense of smell so sharp—are they nature's best sniffers?   67

The HOWs   69

1. How did horses go from tiny creatures to the big animals we know today?   70

2. How do horse breeds differ in their traits and behaviors—what's the secret?   73

3. How does riding a horse work your body—are you getting a sneaky workout?   76

4. How do horses talk to each other with their body language—are their tails telling tales?   78

5. How can we train horses kindly without harsh methods—what's the science behind it?   80

3 | WHY WHAT HUH?!

6. How do horses' eyes let them see almost everything around them—are they the ultimate lookout? 83

7. How do horses use their ears to hear sounds from far away—are they sound pros? 85

8. How does understanding horse behavior help our relationship with them—are we on the same page? 88

9. How does a horse's digestive system work, and why is it so different from ours? 90

10. How do wild horses keep their hooves in shape—are they savvy self-groomers? 93

11. How can you tell if a horse is happy—what signs should we look for? 95

12. How do horses handle different climates—are they nature's ultimate survivors? 98

The WHENs 101

1. When did humans start domesticating horses, and how did it happen? 102

2. When do horses reach full height and weight—do they have a growth spurt? 105

3. When did horses run in the Olympics, and how has it changed over time? 107

4. When did horse racing begin, and why did it become so popular? 109

5. When did horses arrive in the Americas, and how did they impact native cultures? 112

6. When do horses shed their coats, and how does it help them? 115

7. When did the Arabian horse become famous for endurance—what's the backstory? 117

8. When do horses develop their distinct coat patterns—what decides the styles? 120

9. When did shire horses become essential for farming in England—are they true workhorses? 122

10. When did horse therapy come about—how has it changed lives? 125

11. When did the "Renaissance of the Horse" happen, and what got invented? 127

12. When do horses grow rapidly—do they act like teenagers? 130

The HUHs 133

1. Huh?! Did you know horses have different "whinnies" and "neighs," just like we have accents? 134

2. Huh?! Did you know horses can bolt away from danger in seconds—talk about a flight response? 136

3. Huh?! Did you know horses have been friends with humans for over 5,000 years? 138

4. Huh?! Did you know horses can sleep standing up and lying down, depending on how safe they feel? 140

5. Huh?! Did you know the Shire horse is the biggest breed, weighing up to 2,200 pounds—whoa! 142

6. Huh?! Did you know horses can express feelings through facial expressions—watch for their "smiles"! 144

7. Huh?! Did you know the oldest horse lived to be 62 years old—what a senior! 146

8. Huh?! Did you know horses can recognize human faces and remember them for years? 148

9. Huh?! Did you know horse races are often timed to the millisecond—no slacking allowed! 150

10. Huh?! Did you know some horses have allergies—dust, hay, or certain grasses? 153

11. Huh?! Did you know some horses have unique skin patterns called "chrome"—nature's art? 156

12. Huh?! Did you know horses can drink up to 10 gallons of water a day—now that's thirsty! 158

Introduction

Introduction: The Whimsical World of Horses

Welcome to All About Horses! You might think you know these amazing creatures, but get ready for a curiosity adventure! From their powerful hooves thudding against the ground to their gentle whinnies drifting across the fields, horses are much more than just pretty animals. They're social geniuses, skilled communicators, and even caring friends.

Have you ever wondered why these magnificent beings can sleep standing up? Or how they seem to read our feelings? In this book, we'll take a fun stroll through a bunch of surprising questions that reveal the quirky lives of horses. You'll discover astonishing truths about their unique behaviors, dive into the incredible history we share, and learn a few cool tricks about these four-legged pals.

Whether you've ridden horses for years or just love a good horse tale, get ready for a journey that will change how you see the animal world. So, saddle up! Let's gallop down this exciting path of equine discovery. It's time to uncover the answers to all those burning questions and find out what makes horses truly remarkable!

Before Starting

This book is full of fun and curious questions. You don't have to read it from start to finish, just pick what catches your eye in the table of contents. Let your curiosity lead the way!

Follow US

WHY_WHAT_HUH

Join our growing community on Instagram for updates and exciting content. Stay curious with fun facts and engaging posts!

Let a Review!

If you liked the book, we'd love to hear from you! Your review helps us improve and grow. It only takes a minute, and it means a lot to us.

The WHATs

Horses make a landscape look beautiful.

- William Shakespeare

1. What makes a horse's hoof so tough that it thumps the ground without getting damaged?

What makes a horse's hoof so tough that it can thump the ground like a dancing drummer without getting damaged? It's a fun mix of nature's smart design and a few interesting materials!

First, let's look at the hoof itself. Imagine a strong shoe that not only fits perfectly but also absorbs shock like a pro. A horse's hoof is mostly made of keratin, the same stuff in our hair and nails. While your nails might chip after a mishap with a coffee table, the keratin in horse hooves is tightly packed and layered. This gives it incredible strength and durability.

Now, picture a big horse galloping across a field. Each hoof strike creates a huge force—up to 1,500 pounds per square inch! Here's where the hoof's shape becomes important. It's like a rounded cone, helping to spread out this weight evenly. Think of it as a mini trampoline; the more the horse sinks into the ground, the more the hoof bends and absorbs the shock. It makes galloping look so easy!

Then there's the "frog," that squishy, triangular part on the hoof's bottom. It acts like a built-in shock absorber, pumping blood back up through the horse's legs with every step. It's like having a tiny massage therapist right there. This keeps everything flowing smoothly, making sure those strong muscles and bones get all the support they need.

So, the next time you see a horse pounding the ground with its powerful hooves, remember that this tough little structure is a wonder of natural engineering. Designed to take a hit and keep on galloping, it's a great reminder that sometimes the toughest things are also beautifully built. Who needs fancy shoes when you can rock nature's best footwear? Just imagine if we had something similar—running in stilettos would be a breeze!

2. What's the deal with horses sleeping standing up—are they part unicorn?

Horses are those amazing creatures that gallop through our minds and sometimes munch on our garden hoses. They have a cool way of taking a nap—standing up! Now, before you picture a secret unicorn party in the barn, let's explore why horses do this.

First off, horses are prey animals. This means they're often the target for predators. Imagine trying to sleep while a lion is watching you—pretty tough, right? That's where standing up comes in handy. It lets them stay alert and ready to run at a moment's notice. Sleeping while standing is a smart survival tactic.

But how in the world can they pull this off? Enter the stay apparatus. This clever system of tendons and ligaments helps lock their legs in place. It allows them to relax without collapsing. They can snooze on their feet, like experts at a never-ending dance party.

Still, they don't stand up all the time. When they want a deeper sleep—known as REM (Rapid Eye Movement) sleep—they need to lie down. This is when they really dream. Think of them dreaming of green pastures or endless carrots. They only need about 30 minutes of this deep sleep each day, so they sneak in short naps on the ground.

So, while the idea of horses as part-unicorn is delightful—complete with sparkly manes and frolicking in candy-colored fields—the truth is much more practical. They sleep standing for safety, but also find some charming moments of dreamtime when lying down.

In conclusion, horses might not be born from fairy tales, but their special sleep style deserves a round of applause. The next time you see a horse standing quietly in a field, just know that it's likely dreaming of hay bales, not unicorns.

3. What cool tricks do wild horses use to survive out there?

Wild horses are pretty incredible, and they have some clever tricks to survive in the wild. Let's explore a few of these cool strategies.

First, consider their eyes. Wild horses have eyes on the sides of their heads. This gives them an almost panoramic view of their surroundings. They can spot sneaky predators from nearly any direction—like a built-in security camera that never blinks! This sharp eyesight helps them quickly detect danger, so they can make a fast escape when a mountain lion or coyote shows up.

Then there's their social life. Wild horses stick together in groups called harems, where one stallion leads a few mares and their foals. This isn't just for fun or gossip; it's essential for protection. When trouble approaches, the stallion steps up, warning the group and confronting threats. Meanwhile, the mares and foals stay safe in the middle. Teamwork? You bet!

Now, how do they talk to each other? Wild horses are great at communicating with sounds and body language. They snort, whinny, and even kick their hooves. Each sound or move tells the others something important, like "Hello!" or "Get away!" This ability to communicate keeps the herd working together smoothly, helping them navigate new paths or escape danger.

When it comes to food, these horses are the ultimate grazers. They can eat all sorts of plants, which is super handy when their favorites aren't around. They know just what to munch on—grasses, shrubs, you name it! Plus, their tough teeth are perfect for tearing through the fibrous stuff. So, no fancy restaurants here—just good old salad bar grazing!

Lastly, wild horses are incredibly adaptable. They thrive in all kinds of habitats, from hot deserts to wide-open plains. They're like nature's rugged adventurers, always ready to adjust their diets and habits to fit the environment.

In conclusion, wild horses are more than just beautiful creatures running free; they are clever survivalists. With their sharp eyesight, strong sense of community, and flexible diets, they know how to navigate life in the wild. If only we could all be as resourceful as a wild horse. Maybe then we'd gallop through life's challenges, one hoofbeat at a time!

4. What's behind a horse's neigh—do they have their own language?

Behind a horse's neigh lies a rich symphony of sounds that could give Beethoven a run for his money—if he had a soft spot for these magnificent creatures. Horses have their own way of talking, and each neigh, nicker, or whinny is like a little message, bursting with meaning.

Let's break down the neigh. This distinctive sound often means excitement or a wish to connect, a bit like your friend calling you over to join the fun. But here's the twist—it's not just one sound that fits all situations. A high-pitched neigh can mean joy. Meanwhile, a deeper, longer neigh might signal that something's wrong. Think of it like a musical score where each note tells a different tale.

But wait! Horses aren't just about noise. Their body language is essential too. The angle of their ears, the position of their tails, and even how they stand can tell you if they're feeling friendly or a bit standoffish. A prancing horse with perked ears and a swishing tail is likely saying, "Hello, friend! Let's play!" On the flip side, a horse with pinned ears and a tense body might be whispering, "Back off, buddy!"

Ever wonder how horses really chat with one another? Research shows they have an amazing social smarts. They not only communicate with fellow horses but can also read human emotions. They respond differently to a happy face versus a grumpy one. Think of them as the caring friends of the animal kingdom, always tuned in to the vibes around them.

In a nutshell, each neigh and nicker is a little conversation. While they may not have an official horse-to-human phrasebook, they definitely speak their own language. So, the next time you hear a horse neighing, imagine it as a friendly nudge, saying, "Hey, come talk to me!"

To sum up this horsey chat, while we might not fully grasp the depths of their "talking," one thing is clear—when it comes to conversation, horses have a lot to say, even if their "words" come with a side of hay!

5. What's the scoop on where horse coat patterns come from?

Horse coat patterns are like nature's own art gallery—each horse flaunts its unique look. But where do these playful designs come from? Let's trot down this colorful path and uncover the secrets behind those dappled spots, stripes, and swirls.

At the core of this equine fashion show is a mix of genetics and a pinch of evolutionary magic. Each horse carries different genes, like a wardrobe bursting at the seams. These genes decide its coat color and pattern. Will your four-legged friend be dressed in a sleek brown coat, a frosty gray, or maybe a flashy pinto with quirky patches? The choices are endless.

Take the overo and tobiano patterns in the pinto family, for instance. The overo pattern has random white patches that often don't cross the back, while the tobiano displays more even white spots that do. Think of it as an abstract painting versus a smartly arranged checkerboard—both are beautiful but completely different.

The origins of these patterns reach back to the horse's ancestors. They had to adapt to their surroundings in the wild. Some coat patterns help horses blend into the dappled light of a forest, while solid coats might suit the open plains better. It's all about survival in style!

Research into horse coat patterns is ongoing. Scientists are exploring the horse genome to find specific genes responsible for these stunning variations. We can identify some patterns now, but it's like reading a book that's only halfway done—many secrets are still waiting to be discovered.

So, the next time a horse struts by in a breath-taking coat pattern, take a moment to admire the genetic artistry at work. Horses are not just animals; they are walking, trotting canvases of nature's creativity. Who knew beneath those flowing manes and shiny coats lay secrets of genes and evolution, making the equestrian world a bit more colorful? Just shows—sometimes nature's patterns can be as mesmerizing as a beautifully crafted quilt; it's all in the stitching!

6. What can horse behavior teach us about how we interact with each other?

Horses, those majestic four-legged companions that can make even mucking out a stable feel like a royal affair, have a lot to teach us about how we interact with one another. If you've ever watched a herd of horses in a field, you'd see a social life that rivals any reality TV show.

First, let's dive into body language. Horses communicate mainly through movement and posture. Watch closely! When a horse pins its ears back, it's not just a fashion choice; it signals that something's bothering them. This can remind us to pay attention to our friends. If your colleague suddenly goes quiet—or seems more tense than a cat at a dog show—it might be time to check in. Recognizing these signs can help you connect before they trot off into their own thoughts.

Next, consider the idea of hierarchy. Horses naturally group themselves, deciding who is in charge. This isn't just about who gets the best hay; it shows us how important respect and collaboration are in our interactions. Whether it's assigning roles for a project or figuring out who should bring snacks to book club, understanding each other's strengths can make everything run a bit smoother.

Now, let's talk about play. Horses enjoy games, nudging each other and engaging in light-hearted sparring. This playful behavior is a reminder that fun isn't just for kids—it's crucial for building bonds. Think about it: when was the last time you shared a laugh instead of scrolling on your phone? Next gathering, try starting a game. It might just be the spark your group needs!

Finally, let's explore trust. Horses are incredibly sensitive and rely on their connections with humans. Just like a horse will back away if it doesn't trust you, people can be wary too. Building trust among your peers creates a stable environment. A simple smile can work wonders—like a gentle nuzzle from a horse. A little kindness can bridge gaps and strengthen ties.

In conclusion, watching horses can teach us so much about being aware of each other's feelings. They're sensitive to moods and signals—something we can all learn to do better. Next time you're in a group, channel your inner horse: pay attention, respect boundaries, have fun, and don't hesitate to share a friendly nudge. Life is too short to take everything seriously—unless you're crossing a creek with a cranky mare in tow!

7. What role did horses have in building ancient societies that we often overlook?

Horses, those majestic creatures with flowing manes and a knack for munching on your favorite shoes, played a surprisingly crucial role in shaping ancient societies. While we often credit towering monuments or brilliant minds for the rise of civilizations, it's easy to overlook the hoofed heroes that galloped alongside history's most remarkable events.

Let's first talk about transportation. Before we had scooters, and even way before bicycles made their grand entrance, humans had horses. These four-legged friends dramatically improved how quickly and efficiently people could move. Picture this: you're trying to deliver an urgent message across vast lands. Sure, you could walk, but wouldn't you prefer to ride a horse and arrive in style? Thanks to horses, news traveled faster than ever. Rulers could respond to threats and rally troops quickly, changing how societies interacted with one another.

Next up is agriculture. Horses weren't just for sport; they were also hard workers. Their strength made them perfect for plowing fields and moving goods. With horses, ancient farmers could tend to larger plots, producing more food. Think of it as the original grocery delivery service. More food meant more people could settle in one place, leading to the birth of cities and trade routes. That was the spark for complex societies!

Now, let's dive into culture. Horses found their way into stories, religions, and artwork. They symbolized power and nobility. Many cultures, like the Mongols and Celts, wove horses into their identities. These swift creatures inspired myths and legends that still speak to us today. In a way, horses helped shape nations, becoming more than just animals—they were symbols of spirit and drive.

But wait, there's more! Horses also played a sneakily important role in diplomacy. When it came to forming alliances or making peace, a shiny horse often became the ultimate bargaining chip. Imagine trading a trusty steed for an alliance with a neighboring kingdom—like the ancient version of giving someone a brand-new smartphone! Horses helped leaders bond, negotiate deals, and keep the peace (at least until the next horse race broke out).

In wrapping up this equine adventure, it's clear that horses were not just noble steeds running across the plains. They were the unsung heroes of ancient societies. From enhancing communication and agriculture to enriching culture and diplomacy, they truly helped carry humanity forward. So, next time you find yourself watching a Western or admiring a unicorn, remember the mighty horse's understated legacy. It might just inspire you to hop on your bike (or horse) and explore the world with a little more curiosity!

8. What's the surprising reason horses get along with other barn animals?

Horses and barn animals—what a curious mix! At first glance, they might seem like an odd bunch stuck together on a farm. But there's a surprising reason why they get along so well. It all comes down to their social skills and a sprinkle of nature's magic.

Let's dig deeper. Horses are not just pretty faces; they are also social creatures. In the wild, they roam in herds, where getting along is essential. This friendly nature spills over into their relationships with other animals. Horses often feel relaxed around all sorts of barn companions, from sheep to goats to the occasional chicken. Who knew they were so open-minded?

Now, here's where it gets interesting. There's a clever idea called social facilitation. It's a fancy term that means animals thrive when they are with others—especially when they are all happily munching on hay. If one horse makes friends with a pig, you can bet the others will follow. It's like an animal friendship network, but instead of likes, they give each other nibbles!

Speaking of nibbles, let's chat about mutual grooming. This isn't just a spa day for horses, though that would be delightful. Mutual grooming happens when animals help each other out by nibbling at hard-to-reach spots. This back-scratching builds trust and friendship, not just among horses, but across species. So, if a horse meets a donkey, that donkey might just get a little love too!

And here's a fun fact: safety in numbers is a big deal. In the wild, being in a herd helps protect animals from predators. So when different barn animals hang out together, they can keep an eye out for each other. One horse might spot danger—like a sneaky fox—while the goats just keep munching on their hay.

In short, horses get along with other barn animals because they are social, friendly, and perhaps a bit curious. They're like that neighbor who invites everyone over for a barbecue, making sure there's room for all. So, next time you see a horse and a pig sharing a cozy corner in the barn, remember: they're not just barn buddies. They're part of a wonderfully quirky community that makes life on the farm even more delightful!

9. What do horses' problem-solving skills reveal about their smarts?

Horses are often seen as majestic creatures galloping through fields, but they also have some surprising tricks up their sleeves when it comes to solving problems. So, what do these four-legged friends reveal about their smarts? Spoiler: it's more than just "being good at looking pretty."

First off, let's talk about their thinking skills. Research shows that horses can understand cause and effect. They can figure out how to unlock a simple gate or navigate a maze. In one fun experiment, horses chose between two buckets—one with food and the other empty. Pretty clever for a creature that spends much of its day munching!

Now, it's not just about getting the treat. Horses can learn from their mistakes. If a horse tries a problem and doesn't succeed, it adapts. Picture a kid learning to ride a bike: they wobble, fall, and then get back up to try again, each time a little smarter. This ability to adjust shows a type of intelligence that goes beyond simple instincts.

But there's more! Horses are social animals, which adds another layer to their smarts. They often work together, showing they understand social dynamics. Have you seen a horse nudge another to share snacks or comfort a buddy in distress? That's emotional intelligence right there! They can even communicate their needs through body language, which is key when you're a creature that sometimes says, "I'll kick you if you don't move."

Interestingly, studies have shown that horses can pick up on human cues, responding to our gestures and expressions. If you've ever seen a horse tilt its head in confusion while you point at a carrot, you're witnessing that delightful mix of horse smarts and our human knack for miscommunication.

When we put all these pieces together—problem-solving, adaptability, social smarts, and the ability to read humans—it becomes clear: horses are packing some serious brainpower under those flowing manes. They aren't just riding buddies or racing champs;

they're clever creatures navigating a world that's much more complex than we often realize.

So, the next time you spot a horse in a pasture, remember: behind that soulful gaze and gentle demeanor lies a creature that could probably win a few rounds in charades. Whether they're figuring out puzzles or working together in herds, horses remind us that intelligence comes in many forms—even if it sometimes involves a bit of hay. Who knew equine brains could be so fascinating?

10. What's the story behind the phrase "don't look a gift horse in the mouth"?

The phrase "don't look a gift horse in the mouth" is one of those charming bits of wisdom that has trotted through history, and it's pretty intriguing. But what does it really mean, and where did it come from? Let's saddle up and explore the story behind this curious saying.

At its heart, the phrase tells us not to closely examine a gift. If someone hands you a horse, it's probably better to say "thank you" than start checking its teeth. Why focus on horses and dental details?

Horses were essential in the past, and their age and health can be judged by their teeth—older horses often have more worn-down ones. So, if you get a horse as a gift and check its mouth, you might discover it's not exactly the vibrant steed you hoped for. This saying reminds us to appreciate what we receive instead of nitpicking its flaws.

The saying actually goes back to St. Jerome, a Christian scholar from the 4th century. He pointed out that we shouldn't be too critical of gifts. His original Latin version translates to something like "You must not check the teeth of a horse given to you." Fast forward to the 16th century, and voilà! It appears in English literature, becoming a popular phrase.

This wisdom also sheds light on our own thinking. We often feel the urge to doubt or analyze what we receive. Yet, with a gift horse in mind, we're nudged to enjoy the surprise and delight without dissecting it. Sometimes, the joy of a present—a horse, a compliment, or even a cookie—comes from accepting it as it is.

So, the next time you receive something wrapped in the shiny paper of goodwill, remember: it's not just about the thought. It's also about savoring the moment. Embrace that "gift horse" and take a ride into the unknown! Who knows, you might just end up with a great story about almost overthinking a perfectly nice gift. And that, my friend, is the real treasure!

11. What does a horse's mane and tail say about its feelings?

The flowing mane and tail of a horse aren't just for looking fabulous on a sunny day; they also reveal the horse's emotional state. Think of them as a furry version of a person's facial expressions. A horse might not tell you how it feels in words, but its mane and tail certainly have a story to tell.

When a horse is calm and content, you'll often see its mane and tail hanging loosely. Picture it like a casual hairstyle—nothing fancy, just a relaxed vibe. This slinky style shows that the horse feels safe and at ease, perhaps enjoying a nice afternoon of grazing or a visit from its favorite human.

On the flip side, an anxious or scared horse might toss its mane around or hold its tail high. It's like someone having a bad hair day, frantically running their fingers through their locks. When a horse's tail is held high like a flag, it can signal worry or excitement. If the tail is swishing back and forth? Brace yourself—it could mean the horse is annoyed or feeling threatened, much like when someone tries to swat away an irritating fly!

If you notice a horse tucking its tail between its legs or pressing its ears back against its head, it's about as cheerful as a grumpy cat. This position often suggests submission, fear, or discomfort. In horse language, this is like crossing your arms and sulking.

But wait, there's more! Just like we change our hairstyles for special occasions, horses can also style their manes and tails based on their mood. A horse might fluff up its mane when feeling adventurous or even a bit frisky—like putting on a party hat.

So, the next time you see a horse strutting its stuff with its mane flowing like a flag, remember: it's not just about looking majestic. The mane and tail are nature's mood ring, telling the world how that horse is feeling.

In the colorful world of horses, each flick and swish is a reminder that even these majestic creatures have their own ways to express emotions. So, when you feel curious, channel your inner horse whisperer, and try to decode the tail-tales your equine friends have to share. After all, understanding feelings can sometimes be as simple as taking a closer look at the hair!

12. What common horse myths have been busted by science?

When it comes to horses, myths trot alongside them like excited foals. These magnificent creatures are often cloaked in tales, and over time, people have conjured many tall stories about them. But science has stepped in to set the record straight. Let's canter through a few common horse myths that have been debunked.

First on the list is the belief that horses can sleep standing up. It's tempting to picture them as forever alert, always on guard. While horses can doze while standing, thanks to a special locking mechanism in their legs, they still need to lie down for deep sleep. Just like we cherish our cozy beds, horses need their downtime too! Without enough REM sleep, they can become a bit cranky, much like you after too many late nights binge-watching shows.

Next, let's tackle the idea that horses can't see directly in front of them. Imagine a horse squinting like a puzzled librarian trying to read a blurry sign. The truth is, horses have a blind spot right in front of their noses and behind them. But don't fret! They have an impressive field of vision, nearly 360 degrees! So while they may miss that carrot you tossed at their hooves, they can spot a sneaky cat plotting mischief in the corner of the barn.

Now, onto the "one-horsepower" myth. Many folks think a horse equals exactly one horsepower, which sounds neat and tidy. But sadly, this is a bit misleading. The term "horsepower" was coined by James Watt in the 18th century to market steam engines. But in reality, horses can produce anywhere from 10 to 15 horsepower in short bursts. So when you brag about how much you can lift, remember that your equine buddy might be a bit overqualified.

Finally, let's bust the myth that a horse's color tells you something about its personality. While it's fun to think that a chestnut horse is all fire and fury, science finds no link between coat color and behavior. Every horse is a unique mix of personality, training, and experiences. So, just because a horse is a "fiery red" doesn't mean it's a drama queen; it might just be the next star of a Netflix series about equine adventures!

In the end, these myths show us how curiosity leads to greater understanding, whether we're talking about horses or the mysteries of life. So, the next time you find yourself busting myths at the barn or at a dinner party, trot out these insights to impress your friends! Who knows, you might spark a new generation of curious equestrians eager to know more about their four-legged pals.

The WHYs

I can make a General in five minutes but a good horse is hard to replace.

- Alice Walker

1. Why do horses stick together in herds—are they secretly social?

Horses stick together in herds for a bunch of reasons, and it might leave you wondering if they're secretly throwing social gatherings. While there's no evidence of hoofed tea parties, the reasons behind their herd life are all about survival and a sprinkle of social fun.

First up, there's safety in numbers. In the wild, horses are prey animals, which means they often end up on someone's dinner plate. By hanging out in groups, they create a larger, more intimidating crowd. Plus, with more eyes watching for danger, it's easier to spot a sneaky predator coming—be it a hungry lion or, in the case of domesticated horses, the neighbor's overly curious cat.

But wait, there's more to the story! Herds also offer social perks. Horses are expressive creatures. They communicate through body language and sounds, engaging in activities like grooming each other. This builds strong bonds and brings a sense of community—think of it as a cozy group hug, but with a bit more hay and a lot more hoofbeats.

Young horses learn important skills from their older friends. They pick up everything from finding water to galloping in sync. It's school for them, but instead of classrooms, they have fields to frolic in. Not to mention, the herd has its own social structure. There are leaders, often wise older mares, and followers. These roles keep things organized and help everyone work together. It's like a well-run club, but with a lot more mane and tail.

So, do horses secretly enjoy company? Absolutely! They thrive on social ties. It's not just about survival; it's about friendship, learning, and a good dose of fun. Next time you see a group of horses, picture them as a quirky community—grooming, neighing, and perhaps sharing jokes about the humans who admire them from the fence.

In conclusion, horses are not just herd animals; they're social beings full of life. While they may not host tea parties, they definitely know how to create a warm and supportive group right out in nature. Who knows? Maybe they're even planning their next event—perhaps a hay bale picnic? Now that's one gathering you wouldn't want to miss!

2. Why do some horses seem to sense our feelings—what's their secret?

Horses have a special talent for sensing our feelings, almost like they have their own emotional radar. So, what's their secret? Let's dive into this fascinating world together!

First off, horses are social animals. They live in herds, which means they've become experts at reading body language and subtle signals. Think of it as their own school of non-verbal communication, where they've learned to interpret everything from a flick of an ear to the position of a tail. When you feel anxious or happy, your body gives off hints—like changes in your posture or breath. Horses, with their sharp senses, can pick up on these clues. It's as if they have front-row seats to the human story unfolding in front of them!

But there's even more! Horses can also detect pheromones—those invisible chemical signals we release when we experience emotions. When you're stressed, your body might let out certain scents that let a horse know how you're feeling. It's like they're perfume detectives, sniffing out the unique aroma of your emotional state! Who knew we had such fragrant giveaways?

Let's not forget the deep connection that can form between humans and horses. Many riders and trainers talk about a special bond that's built on respect and understanding. This connection creates a kind of feedback loop: your feelings influence the horse's actions, and their reactions can change how you feel. A calm horse might ease your worries, while a spirited one might kick your excitement into high gear. It's a two-way street of emotional sharing!

In the big picture, horses are like four-legged therapists. They seem to know that humans can be a bit confusing. Their ability to sense feelings isn't about mind-reading; it's about being in tune with their surroundings and the people in them. So, next time a horse gazes at you with those big, soulful eyes, remember—they're probably just trying to figure out if you need a friendly cuddle or a calming moment.

So, what's the takeaway? Horses might not be able to put our emotions into words, but their amazing skills in observation help them connect with us in surprising ways. Next time you're feeling down, consider having a heart-to-heart with your equine friend—they just might be the best listeners you'll ever meet!

3. Why are some horses more unique in personality—does mood matter?

Horses are amazing creatures, galloping through fields with grace. But here's the twist: each horse has its own personality, some bursting with energy, while others seem content to chill in the shade. So, what makes some horses stand out like stars in a movie while others blend into the background? Let's explore!

First up, genetics. Just like people, horses have a mix of genes that shape their traits. You see, some horses may be born with a naturally curious spirit, while others hang back a bit. Breeds play a part too! For instance, Arabians are known for their lively personalities, while Percherons tend to be more relaxed. It's like how some friends are always the life of the party, while others prefer a quiet evening with a good book.

Next, let's talk about the environment. A horse raised in a lively setting—lots of companions, new activities, and plenty of love—will likely be more outgoing. In contrast, a horse that has faced isolation or rough handling might be cautious, or even a bit dramatic in new situations. Consider how your friends' moods can change the vibe of an outing; a horse's experiences shape how it interacts with the world too.

And there's more! Research shows that horses feel a range of emotions. From joy to anxiety, these feelings can influence their behavior. A happy horse may prance around, while a stressed one holds back. It's all about how they see their surroundings, just like how you might react to a surprise party or a surprise exam.

So, when we dive into the world of horse personalities, it's a delightful mix of genetics, environment, and emotions. Each horse tells its own story, adding a unique twist to life in the barn. The next time you meet a horse with a big personality or a gentle soul, remember: they aren't just four-legged friends; they're reflections of their unique journeys.

In the end, maybe we could learn a thing or two about embracing our quirks from these wonderful creatures. After all, every horse is a character in the grand tale of life, and isn't that a story worth sharing?

4. Why do horses have great memories—can they recall a ride from years ago?

Horses, those stunning creatures with flowing manes and a knack for munching hay, are not just pretty sights trotting around the paddock. They boast remarkable memory skills that would make even an elephant raise an eyebrow—if elephants had eyebrows, that is. So, why do these four-legged friends have such great memories?

Let's peek inside a horse's brain. It's not just an impressive hat rack; it's filled with neurons that help them remember experiences, much like we hold onto that one embarrassing karaoke night. Horses can recall rides, locations, and even the not-so-friendly stable cat they met years ago. Research shows that horses have excellent associative memory, meaning they remember events linked to specific experiences. If a horse had a thrilling gallop down a favorite trail or not-so-fun times during a thunderstorm, you bet they'll hang onto those memories for a while.

One cool fact? Horses can recognize their humans even after long absences. This explains why your mare prances with joy when she sees you after a week away. She's not just excited about the carrots you're holding; she's remembering all the fun rides you've shared. Their memory isn't only about recalling past events. It's about recognizing patterns and making smart decisions based on what they've learned. So if a horse discovers that stepping into a muddy field leads to a sticky situation, it might just avoid that mess next time. Talk about holding a grudge!

While we might not all have a photographic memory, horses excel at a unique skill: living in the moment while also remembering their past. When you hop on for a ride, your horse might be pulling up memories of the last exhilarating journey you took together, reliving every joyful moment while eagerly anticipating what lies ahead.

To wrap it all up, horses have great memories because they're wired to remember experiences as a survival tool. In the wild, knowing which areas are safe and which ones are risky can make the difference between a peaceful munch and a sudden sprint. So the next time you ride, remember this: your equine friend might just be reminiscing about all the adventures you've had together. And who knows? They might even be plotting your next thrilling escapade or just enjoying the twists and turns of your journey. It's a beautiful bond built on memory—and maybe, just a dash of mischief!

5. Why do certain breeds shine in specific sports—what's the reason?

Certain dog breeds stand out in specific sports, and while it might seem like they've been training with a canine Olympian, there's a mix of genetics, history, and a touch of fabulous personality at play.

Let's start with genetics. Just like how some people can effortlessly shoot hoops while others trip over their own feet, different breeds have been specially bred for certain traits. Take Border Collies, for example. They are the top achievers of the dog world. With their smart brains and a desire to please, they're perfect for agility sports. Their herding instincts push them to chase and control, making them experts at navigating obstacle courses. They seem to be born to zig-zag through tunnels!

Next up, we have the enthusiastic Labrador Retrievers. These furry friends seem made for fetching things. With their webbed feet and strong bodies, they are the stars of doggy dock diving competitions. You might say they are the Michael Phelps of the canine pool.

But it's not just about physical traits. Training and socialization matter, too. Many sporting dogs, like Spaniels, have been working alongside humans for ages. This teamwork builds a strong bond and makes them eager to learn. They don't see us just as owners; they see us as partners in fun, ready to chase after a frisbee or herd sheep.

Let's not overlook personality! Some breeds have a playful spark, like Beagles bouncing around in the field, sniffing every blade of grass. Their curiosity fuels their love for activities, while their determination makes them little athletes.

In the end, it's a joyful mix of traits, history, feelings, and a sprinkle of fun that explains why certain breeds shine in specific sports. It's like being born with a shiny tennis ball in their mouth, rather than just luck. So, next time you see a dog in the spotlight at a sporting event, remember: it's not just about chance; it's pedigree, personality, and a bit of puppy enthusiasm that makes them champions. After all, who wouldn't want to chase their dreams—or that frisbee flying through the sky—while being cheered on?

6. Why are horses labeled "cold-blooded" or "hot-blooded"—what does it mean?

Horses come in all shapes and sizes, and they have some intriguing labels that might make them seem a bit dramatic. We're talking about "cold-blooded" and "hot-blooded." No, this doesn't mean they're part of some bizarre equine showdown. It's all about temperament and ancestry, with a sprinkle of biology thrown in for good measure!

Let's take a stroll down the horse family tree. "Hot-blooded" horses—like speedy Arabians and fiery Thoroughbreds—are known for their lively nature. Think of them as the race cars of the horse world. They're energetic and quick to react. A flick of their tail or a twitch of their ears signals excitement or impatience. Hot-blooded actually hints at their ability to be lively and responsive, much like a turbocharged engine ready to roar.

On the other side of the pasture, we have the "cold-blooded" horses, such as the gentle Clydesdales and sturdy Percherons. They're the easy-going pals who prefer a leisurely stroll to a sprint. This doesn't mean they're lazy. They're just steady, strong, and great for work or relaxing rides. Think of them as the dependable SUVs of the horse world, always ready for a family trip—or a cozy hayride.

These terms come from history. Cold-blooded horses typically descended from heavier breeds used for hard work, while hot-blooded horses were bred for speed and endurance. It's like comparing a cozy winter sweater to a breezy summer t-shirt: both are great, just made for different occasions!

In essence, it's all about temperament and traits rather than actual blood temperature. So next time you see a horse galloping joyfully in the field or plodding along at a slow pace, remember—they're simply showing off their unique personalities.

Which type is better? Well, that depends on what you want! If you crave excitement and energy, a hot-blooded horse might be your best bet. But if you seek a calm, steady companion, a cold-blooded horse may just be the match for you.

So, whether they're "hot" or "cold," horses are a wonderful mix of hoof prints on this curious journey called life! Who knows what adventures await with these fascinating creatures by your side?

7. Why do horses nuzzle and groom each other—just friendly, or more?

When you see horses nuzzling and grooming each other, it looks like something out of a heartwarming movie about best buddies. But there's more to it than just a friendly scene. This behavior is about social bonding, grooming, and a bit of horsey etiquette!

Why do they do it? Horses are social animals, like us at a crowded coffee shop, chatting and making plans. When they nuzzle and groom, they strengthen their connections—think of it as a warm group hug, minus the clumsy arm placements.

Now, let's break it down. Grooming helps establish hierarchies in the herd, serving as a friendly reminder of who's in charge. It's also practical! Horses use grooming to get rid of annoying bugs and dirt. It's a little like helping a friend with that stubborn piece of spinach stuck in their teeth: a helpful act that says, "I care about you!"

But there's more! Horses communicate a lot with body language. A gentle nuzzle shows calmness and trust. Picture one horse leaning in, saying, "I've got your back!" It's a sweet reminder that they're in this together.

So, is it just friendly? Not quite. It's a delightful mix of friendship, social order, and caring vibes—a lively dance that makes horse society work. Imagine if humans enjoyed a grooming session daily; those office water cooler chats would turn into something else entirely!

In short, the next time you see a horse giving its buddy a nuzzle, remember this: they're not just sharing affection; they're creating strong bonds, keeping clean, and showing trust. In the world of horses, it's more than a friendly nuzzle; it's a beautiful testament to friendship, teamwork, and a bit of practical grooming. Now that's a story worth sharing!

8. Why can we tell a horse's age and health by its teeth—are they nature's age detectors?

Horses, those magnificent animals galloping through fields, have a secret that could outshine even the best birthday party planner: their teeth! That's right—those pearly whites are little detectives when it comes to figuring out a horse's age and health. So, are they nature's age detectors? Let's dive into this idea.

Horses don't get fancy birthday parties every year. Instead, their teeth tell us how long they've been trotting on this Earth. Just like how your favorite book ages—getting a bit dog-eared and yellowed, but filled with stories! Horses start off with baby teeth, which they lose as they grow up. By around five years old, they have their adult teeth in place.

Veterinarians and horse experts become like dental detectives, examining signs like the shape, wear, and even some unique ridges or hooks. It's like playing a specialized game of "Guess Who?" but with teeth. Pretty neat, huh?

But there's even more! Just like a well-worn pair of shoes, a horse's teeth show signs of wear over time, revealing their health. If a horse's teeth are worn down to nubs, it could mean they're quite old and might struggle to graze—or maybe they just had a serious love affair with carrots!

When a vet peeks inside a horse's mouth, they look for important clues: the size and shape of the teeth, how they fit together, and any signs of dental problems. A healthy set of chompers means a happy, lively horse, ready to trot into the sunset without a care in the world.

In conclusion, while we might not throw a party just by checking a horse's teeth, they have a lot to say! Next time you come across a horse, remember their teeth are nature's very own age detectors. Who knew something so simple could reveal so much? It's a delightful surprise, much like discovering hidden clues in your favorite mystery novel!

9. Why is horse therapy becoming a go-to for helping people?

Horse therapy, or equine-assisted therapy, is galloping into the spotlight as a top choice for helping people tackle all sorts of challenges, from mental health struggles to developmental issues. But why are these magnificent creatures becoming the go-to therapists? Let's saddle up and find out!

First off, horses are fantastic listeners. They might not nod in sympathy, but they can sense human emotions better than most people. Their amazing ability to read body language means they respond to feelings in ways even the best human therapists can't match. Picture this: you share your worries with a horse, and it responds with a soft nuzzle or a calming huff. It's like having a therapist who doesn't judge, occasionally munches hay, and has a mane that could win awards.

Scientifically speaking, interacting with horses releases feel-good hormones—endorphins and oxytocin. These are your body's natural mood lifters. Spending time with these gentle giants often leads to more relaxation and happiness. Plus, taking care of a big, powerful animal can really boost your self-esteem. When you can guide a horse around a ring, you begin to feel like you can tackle just about anything life throws at you. Talk about a confidence boost!

What's truly special about horse therapy is that it often involves hands-on activities like grooming, riding, or just strolling beside these friendly creatures. This engaging approach can be especially helpful for people who have a tough time with traditional talk therapy. For many, just being near a horse is calming—almost like a furry form of mindfulness.

And think about it: horses have been our companions for thousands of years. They've walked with us through history—working on farms, serving in wars—and now they're stepping into the role of emotional support. That's a remarkable evolution!

In conclusion, horse therapy is becoming popular not just because it's enjoyable and soothing, but also because it combines emotional support with physical activity. So, the next time you're feeling down, why not consider a 'mane' squeeze instead of a regular therapy session? After all, who wouldn't want to share their feelings with a horse that has the patience of a saint and a personality full of charm? It's a unique ride towards healing!

10. Why do horses kick—what's behind this instinct?

Horses are fascinating creatures that gallop through our imaginations and fill our hearts with wonder. One of their curious behaviors? Kicking. If you've ever been on the receiving end of a horse's swift hind leg—a situation most of us would prefer to avoid—you might be asking, "What's behind this surprising move?"

At its core, a horse kicks for a few key reasons. It's like their version of self-defense or a not-so-subtle way of communicating. First, think about this: horses are prey animals. Unlike your average housecat that is more about plotting its next nap, horses have evolved to be hyper-aware of threats. When they sense danger—sometimes as harmless as an annoying fly or something truly scary—they might kick. It's their way of saying, "Not today, pesky predator!" or, in a more amusing light, "Take that, unwelcome bug!"

But kicking isn't just about fending off foes. It can also be a sign of joy or irritation. Imagine a horse at play, frolicking with a buddy and delivering a light kick for fun. It's like a horsey high-five—just with a lot more hoof and less grace! On the flip side, if a horse kicks out while you're grooming it or doesn't want you close, it's saying, "Personal space, please!" They have their own unique way of socializing, and sometimes, that includes a swift hoof.

Here's something cool: kicking is instinctual. It's a behavior that's built into their DNA, shaped by millions of years of evolution. It's a tool for survival, a playful gesture, and a way to communicate, all wrapped into one amazing package of hooves and muscle.

So, the next time you see a horse, remember this: behind those big, soulful eyes lies a history of instincts and behaviors that make them endlessly fascinating. And if a horse gives a little kick, it might just be trying to remind you of something important. Even the mightiest creatures can have a sense of humor. After all, who can resist a little kick of curiosity?

11. Why do some horses bond more closely with humans than with each other?

Horses are truly fascinating creatures. Their relationships can be a bit like a high school drama—full of cliques and unexpected friendships. So why do some horses bond more closely with humans than with their fellow horse buddies? Let's take a curious trot down this path together.

First, let's think about the horse's natural instincts. Horses are herd animals. They thrive on social interactions with their own kind—think of it as their version of a Netflix binge party. But sometimes, a horse finds a human more appealing than its horse pals. If a horse spends a lot of time with people during its early days, it starts to see humans as safe and comforting. And let's not forget those delicious carrots! Who wouldn't want to hang out with someone who brings snacks?

Another important point is that horses are incredibly sensitive. They can read human emotions and body language much like we read a best-selling novel. When a human is calm, consistent, and caring, a horse begins to trust them. It's like finding that perfect book you can't put down. In contrast, other horses can be unpredictable, leading some to seek out the reliability of humans.

Then there's the fun aspect of training and interaction. Horses that enjoy activities like riding or groundwork often develop a strong connection with their humans. It's a bit like hitting it off with a teammate after scoring the winning goal. The horse learns to trust the human, leading to that heartwarming bond we all envy.

Let's not forget the individual personalities, too. Just as people have introverts and extroverts, so do horses. Some horses might simply prefer the company of humans, choosing cozy chats instead of joining a noisy herd.

In the end, it's a mix of upbringing, trust, training, and personality that creates those special human-horse bonds. So, the next time you see a horse nuzzling up to its human, remember: it's not just about the carrots—it's about connection.

In the world of horses, sometimes it's more fun to be the designated driver on a leisurely gallop than the passenger in an equine party bus. And who could blame them? After all, humans just know how to throw a better party!

12. Why is a horse's sense of smell so sharp—are they nature's best sniffers?

Horses have a remarkable sense of smell—one that could give even the most seasoned bloodhound a run for its money. But what's behind this amazing talent? Let's trot down this aromatic path of curiosity.

First, let's talk numbers. Horses have about 350 different scent receptors in their noses, while humans only have around 5 million. Yes, you read that right. If horses were at a fancy dinner party, they'd be the guests savoring every aroma while we're just trying to figure out if the green stuff is salad or something that got left behind. This keen sense of smell helps horses find food, spot friends and foes, and even pick up on emotions from other horses. They're like big, fuzzy detectives on four legs, sniffing out clues in their world.

But that's not all. Horses have a special trick up their noses: the vomeronasal organ, or Jacobson's organ. This little wonder helps them analyze pheromones—those tiny scent signals that tell horses who's who in the herd. It's a built-in social media feed for sniffing out the latest gossip. When a horse catches a whiff of another horse's sweat, it can tell if that horse is feeling frisky or scared—more accurately than our mood rings ever could!

So why is a horse's sense of smell so sharp? Evolution, my friend! In the wild, it's a matter of survival. Detecting predators from a distance can mean the difference between munching grass peacefully and sprinting away in a panic. Since horses can't just flick on a light or call for help, a strong sniffer is their best alarm system.

To top it off, horses can recognize their human friends not just by sight or sound, but by the unique mix of scents we all carry. So next time you're bonding with a horse, remember: they're sniffing out your soul, one whiff at a time.

In conclusion, while you might be tempted to crown horses the champions of sniffing, don't forget about other impressive creatures. Snakes, dogs, and even certain insects have their own olfactory talents. However, when you consider their social skills, survival instincts, and sharp sense of smell, horses certainly deserve a spot on the podium with a shiny medal that reads "World's Best Sniffer." After all, in the grand sniff-off of nature, they're definitely ahead of the pack!

The HOWs

There's something about the outside of a horse that is good for the inside of a man.

- Abraham Lincoln

1. How did horses go from tiny creatures to the big animals we know today?

Horses have had quite the makeover over millions of years—think of it as the ultimate evolution fitness journey. Let's saddle up and explore how these magnificent creatures turned from tiny, dainty beings into the powerful animals we admire today.

First stop on our timeline: way back around 55 million years ago. Picture a horse the size of a house cat. Its name? Eohippus, which sounds like it could be a dinosaur's cousin, but it isn't. This little critter had a slender body, four toes on each foot, and dined on soft leaves and fruits in lush forests. It was more like a snack-sized horse than a majestic steed!

Fast forward millions of years, and our four-legged friends faced a big challenge. As the planet transformed from dense forests to open grasslands, these early horses had to step up their game. They needed to sprint away from hungry predators. So, they began to grow bigger and faster. Imagine upgrading from a bike to a sports car—definitely necessary when a predator is on your tail!

These new horses became larger and developed a single hoof. Why? A strong hoof was much better for galloping across wide plains than tiny toes. Plus, a bigger body could store more energy for sprinting. Talk about a smart evolution strategy!

Next came Hipparion, about 12 million years ago. This creature looked like a mini version of today's horse. Picture a sleek, speedy companion that could outrun the fastest mailman. But even with this upgrade, horses still had to compete with other fast animals. So, nature kept fine-tuning them, leading to the strong, majestic horses we see today.

As they galloped through time, horses became crucial to human societies. They helped us plow fields and carried us on adventures. Don't forget, they've also starred in sports, racing, and therapy—what a glow-up!

So, how did horses go from small, timid creatures to the grand animals we ride today? It's a journey of survival, change, and a sprinkle of trial and error. If only we could all evolve as gracefully! Next time you see a horse, remember: it's not just a pretty face; it's a wonder of millions of years of evolution. It's a story of resilience and strength. So whether you're riding one or admiring it from afar, keep in mind that they didn't get where they are without hard work and plenty of galloping!

2. How do horse breeds differ in their traits and behaviors—what's the secret?

Horse breeds are like a chocolate box of the equestrian world—each one uniquely crafted with traits that make them deliciously different. Whether you're eyeing a sprightly Thoroughbred or a sturdy Clydesdale, there's a fascinating recipe behind each breed's personality and behavior. So, what's the secret sauce? Let's trot down this trail of curiosity together.

First up, we have genetics. This is the blueprint that defines each breed. Imagine each horse as a unique snowflake. Thanks to selective breeding over centuries, different breeds have developed distinct characteristics. Some horses, like Arabians, have been bred for stamina and agility, making them the athletes of the horse kingdom. Others, like the heavyset Percheron, are designed for strength and pulling power, perfect for plowing fields or pulling carriages. Different goals, different horses.

But it's not just about their looks. Behavior is also influenced by how horses have been raised and trained. A spirited Thoroughbred might be a bit of a diva—full of energy and a competitive spirit—while the laid-back Quarter Horse tends to be more easygoing and adaptable. One is not better than the other; each shows how experiences shape their personalities.

The environment matters, too. Horses that live in a busy ranch with lots of action might be more alert and social. In contrast, those in a quiet pasture often have a more relaxed vibe. So, in a way, horses are like us—our surroundings influence how we behave and interact with the world.

Now, don't forget about instincts. Horses are prey animals, meaning they've developed a healthy sense of caution. Some breeds may be more skittish (looking at you, Arabian), while others are grounded and calm (hello, Haflinger). This instinctual behavior can vary widely across breeds, adding to their overall character.

In summary, the secret to how horse breeds differ lies in genetics, upbringing, and instincts—a colorful mix of traits. So next time you see a horse, remember that there's a whole world of history behind that beautiful face. Each breed tells a story, and it's up to us to listen with curious hearts. Who knows? Maybe the next horse you meet will share its secrets—and perhaps even become a new friend along the way!

3. How does riding a horse work your body—are you getting a sneaky workout?

Riding a horse might look like a simple, relaxing way to spend your afternoon. After all, you're sitting on a big, beautiful animal, right? But let's dig a little deeper: you might just be getting a sneaky workout without even realizing it!

First up, let's talk about your core muscles. These little champions of stability work hard when you ride. As the horse moves, your body has to adjust to keep you balanced. So while you're enjoying the breeze on your face, your deep abdominal muscles are busy trying to keep you upright. Think of it as a fancy core exercise, like doing pilates while sitting on a living creature!

Next comes your leg strength. When you ride, your thighs and calves are gripping the horse. This isn't just for show; it's a workout! Your leg muscles are contracting and relaxing to stay connected to your four-legged friend. It's leg day in disguise—no sweaty gym required.

Now, let's chat about your upper body. While your lower half is working hard, your arms and shoulders are engaged too. You need to control the reins, which requires steady arms and good posture. All this adds up to a great way to strengthen your upper body while looking cool and collected. Who knew horse riding could help you tone those shoulders?

Don't forget the cardio! If you've ever galloped down a trail or even just trotted around in a ring, you know your heart is pumping. Riding gets your heart rate up, especially with those faster moves. It's like a jog, but with a fabulous equine companion.

So yes, biking to the barn is one thing, but riding is a whole other level. You could become a fitness fan without ever stepping foot in a gym. Plus, there's something magical about the bond between you and your horse. That connection not only strengthens your body but also lifts your spirits, lowering stress and boosting happiness.

In conclusion, the next time someone asks if you've really exercised while riding, you can proudly say: "Absolutely! I'm not just horsing around!" So saddle up and enjoy those unexpected fitness benefits—you might discover that your "sneaky workout" is the most fun you'll ever have staying fit!

4. How do horses talk to each other with their body language—are their tails telling tales?

Horses are like the original body language experts—no words needed! Instead of chatting about the weather or their favorite hay, they use a whole set of moves and expressions to show how they feel. If you've ever watched a group of horses in a field, you might wonder: Are their tails telling tales?

Let's start with the tails. A horse's tail can indeed tell stories! When a horse swishes its tail back and forth, it usually means, "I'm annoyed!" It might be fighting off those pesky flies. But if the tail is held high and flicking playfully? That's a sign of excitement or happiness—a joyful flag waving in the breeze.

But the tail isn't the only player in this silent communication game. Horses use their ears like radar antennas. Picture this: if one ear is pointed forward while the other is turned back, the horse is saying, "I'm curious but cautious!" It's like a kid trying to pay attention in class while eyeing the playground.

Facial expressions are equally important. A horse pinning its ears back or wrinkling its nostrils is sending a clear message: "I'm not happy right now!" On the flip side, soft, relaxed ears and a gentle look in their eye usually mean the horse is calm and content—perhaps plotting their next nap!

Let's not forget about posture. A horse standing tall with its head held high is full of confidence. But a horse that's hunched over? That might be feeling a bit sick or insecure. It's all about the vibe they give off.

Next time you're at the stables or in a pasture, watch closely. Tune in to these equine conversations. You may discover that horses don't just talk to each other—they're quietly sharing tales of friendship, fear, and fun—all without uttering a word. It turns out that horses really do have a lot to say if you know how to listen!

5. How can we train horses kindly without harsh methods—what's the science behind it?

Training horses kindly is like mastering a delicate dance—one where both partners move together, rather than just one trying to lead with a heavy boot. Let's trot through the science of gentle training methods!

First, it's important to remember that horses are very social creatures. They're not just our four-legged pals; they're smart, emotional beings. Think of them as the introverts of the animal kingdom—always observing and sometimes judging us. That means training a horse kindly is all about building trust and clear communication, instead of using harsh methods. No one wants a grumpy horse!

Now, let's put on our science hats. Research shows that horses learn best through positive reinforcement. This is like giving them a tasty treat every time they do something right. A little snack, a gentle pat, or even cheerful words can encourage them to repeat their good behavior. This creates a happy cycle: the horse tries new things, gets rewarded, and soon enough, they're prancing around like they own the place!

On the flip side, harsh training methods—like pulling on a bit or using physical punishment—can create fear and anxiety. A frightened horse is about as useful as a bicycle to a fish. Studies prove that stress hurts a horse's ability to learn. So, a happy horse is a learning horse—this isn't just a feel-good statement; it's science!

One fascinating idea in this gentle approach is called "equine ethology," which is just a fancy way of saying the study of horses in their natural setting. By watching wild horses, trainers have learned that these animals thrive on social interaction and clear signals. Imagine bringing snacks to a party; it's not just about food, but the fun of sharing. Similarly, trainers can achieve so much more by creating a joyful atmosphere where horses feel safe and loved.

A great way to use this science in training is through groundwork exercises. It's where humans and horses work together to build trust. Activities like liberty work or circle work can be enjoyable and enlightening for both. Think of it as a trust fall; it's about knowing that neither party will drop the other.

In conclusion, training horses kindly is all about offering a carrot—not wielding a stick. By understanding the science of horse behavior and choosing positive reinforcement, we create a bond with our equine friends. Plus, we add a splash of fun!

So the next time you find yourself with a horse, remember: a little curiosity, some patience, and a whole lot of kindness can turn training into a delightful dance instead of a choreographed catastrophe. Let's get ready to canter into the wild blue yonder!

6. How do horses' eyes let them see almost everything around them—are they the ultimate lookout?

Horses are wonders of nature, especially when it comes to their eyes. Imagine being able to see almost everything around you without needing to twist your head like a pretzel. That's the life of a horse!

Their large, expressive eyes are positioned on the sides of their heads, giving them an incredible view—around 350 degrees of vision! It's like having your own security camera that never needs recharging. They can see in front, behind, and even to the side, but there's a small blind spot right in front of their nose and behind their tails. Talk about the ultimate lookout!

Now, let's dive a little deeper into the science. Horses have what's called "monocular" vision. This means each eye can focus on different things at once. Picture being at a party, chatting with one friend while keeping an eye on the snack table and the door for new arrivals. That's a horse for you!

But there's a catch. While their wide view is great for spotting predators, their color vision is, well, a bit limited. Horses see mainly in shades of blue and yellow. So, they might notice a rustling bush but could miss that vibrant rainbow at the end of the field.

Their amazing vision isn't the only thing that makes them great at keeping watch. Horses also have fast reflexes and sharp instincts. When they spot something unusual—a moving shadow, a sneaky fox—they can react quickly. They might gallop away or stand firm, ready to assess the situation.

In the grand scheme of things, a horse's vision is crucial for survival. It keeps them alert, ready for surprises, and prepared for a quick getaway, much like that friend who knows just when to leave a party.

So, the next time you see a horse, give them a nod of respect. They're not just beautiful creatures; they're also nature's ultimate lookouts, observing their world with eyes wide open. Isn't that what makes them truly magnificent?

7. How do horses use their ears to hear sounds from far away—are they sound pros?

Horses are those majestic creatures galloping gracefully through fields, radiating a vibe that feels wise. You might wonder: how do their floppy, expressive ears help them hear sounds from far away? Are they some kind of sound pros?

Let's dive in. Horses have evolved ears that work like radar dishes. Their ears can swivel a full 180 degrees, allowing them to catch sounds from all directions without moving their heads. It's like they have a personal sound system, ready to pick up whispers from across the pasture or the soft rustle of leaves miles away!

But there's more. Horses have large, funnel-shaped ears that funnel sounds directly into their ears. This makes them really good at amplifying noises—like they're saying, "Hey, is that a distant rustle of grass? Let's turn it up!" They can hear a wide range of sounds, from 14 Hz to 25 kHz. In simple terms, they can hear higher frequencies than us humans, whose range tops out around 20 kHz. So, while you might think your favorite song is a masterpiece, a horse could be jamming to the subtle sounds of nature instead.

Horses also alert each other to potential dangers using their ears. They tilt them toward a sound while keeping their bodies relaxed. This non-verbal communication is like an equine secret code, helping keep the herd safe from lurking predators. Imagine a horse turning its ear and saying, "Did you hear that? I think there's a snack... or maybe a lion. Let's stay alert."

So, are horses sound pros? In a way, yes! They have the tools to hear sounds from far and wide. They use this ability smartly to navigate their world. Their ears aren't just for flapping in the breeze; they're precision listening devices. They help make the sounds of the wild more harmonious.

Next time you spot a horse standing tall, ears perked up, remember: it's not just listening to the wind or pondering life. It's on high alert, ready to catch what's happening in the great beyond—while probably thinking about when it'll get its next treat. After all, in the world of horses, every sound could lead to adventure... or an irresistible carrot!

8. How does understanding horse behavior help our relationship with them—are we on the same page?

Understanding horse behavior is like cracking a fun code. Once you do, it opens the door to a world of connection. Think of it this way: horses communicate through body language, sounds, and even the flick of an ear. They might not be sending you a text, but they are definitely trying to chat.

When we get what our four-legged friends are saying, we uncover the secrets to a better bond. For instance, if a horse is tossing its head or pinning its ears back, it's not just putting on a show; it's saying something is wrong. On the flip side, a relaxed horse with soft eyes and a swishing tail is inviting you over.

Recognizing these signals helps us respond the right way. This means we are not just two ships passing in the night, but two pals enjoying a sunny day.

Science backs this up, too! A study in "Frontiers in Psychology" shows that horses respond better to humans who pay attention to their body language. This isn't just fluff. Understanding their feelings can make training easier and reduce stress for both horse and rider. It's a win-win!

So, are we on the same page? That really depends on how well we're reading. If we ignore their cues or misread their signals, it's like trying to have a deep chat with someone who speaks a different language. Frustrating, right? But when we tune in, we can build trust and respect. And remember, fewer surprises mean fewer unexpected "conversations" about what's okay in the saddle.

In conclusion, developing curiosity about horse behavior isn't just for the equestrians out there. It's for anyone who wants to join the horse-human book club—one where the reading material is rich with understanding and the discussions are lively (but don't expect any hoofed members to chip in). So the next time you're near a horse, remember: they're just as curious about you as you should be about them. Who knows? You might find you've been on the same page all along; it was just written in hoof prints!

9. How does a horse's digestive system work, and why is it so different from ours?

When it comes to digestion, horses are the graceful dancers of the animal kingdom, all elegance and efficiency but with a few quirky differences compared to our somewhat clumsy human routine. Let's saddle up and trot through the fascinating world of how horses digest their food!

First, the basics. Horses are herbivores, which means they eat only plants. Unlike humans, who can munch on just about anything, horses feast on hay, grass, and grains. Our digestive system is like a straightforward assembly line: we munch, our stomach churns, and eventually, things come out the other end. Simple enough, right?

But horses don't have the same setup. Their journey starts in the mouth, where they chew their food with lots of enthusiasm. Next, things get interesting. Instead of a small stomach like ours, a horse has a relatively small stomach for its size—about the size of a basketball. This little guy can only hold around 2-4 gallons of food at once. So, when it comes to feasting, horses prefer to nibble and graze throughout the day. It's like having a buffet that's always open!

From the stomach, the food—now a mushy mix called chyme—moves into the small intestine. Here, about 70% of nutrient absorption happens. Picture this as the horse's version of a busy marketplace where all the good stuff—proteins, vitamins, and minerals—gets gathered up to nourish its strong body.

But here's where things really get interesting: after the small intestine, the food heads into the large intestine, which is a remarkable structure. It includes the cecum and colon, and together they can hold up to 30 gallons of material! This is like the horse's own fermentation chamber, where helpful bacteria step in to break down tough plant parts. Imagine a cozy potluck where the bacteria digest the pieces we can't handle, making the most of every last bit of that hay. This slow process allows time for nutrients to be absorbed.

So, why is this digestive setup so different from ours? It's all about evolution and diet. Humans have evolved to eat a varied diet that needs quick digestion—thus our efficient stomachs. Horses, on the other hand, are built to thrive on high-fiber diets that need a slower, more thorough approach to digestion.

In short, while we might dash from meal to meal, horses savor the art of nibbling and digesting at a leisurely pace. They're perfectly adapted to their diet. The next time you see a horse munching away in a field, remember: it's not just snacking! It's a masterclass in how to digest food.

Next time you take a bite of your lunch, think about this: somewhere, a horse is munching grass, taking its time, and hoping no one charges them for every nibble. After all, good things come to those who wait, especially in the world of equine digestion!

10. How do wild horses keep their hooves in shape—are they savvy self-groomers?

Wild horses are nature's hoof maintenance pros. They might not have personal grooming kits, but oh, do they know how to keep those hooves in great shape! Imagine a herd of wild horses racing across the plains, their hooves pounding like a drum. Beneath all that power lies a captivating story of self-care.

Let's dive into the hoof itself. A horse's hoof is a wonder of nature made of layers of tough keratin—similar to what makes your hair and nails, but bulkier. In the wild, a horse's active lifestyle is like a gym for its hooves. As they roam over different terrains, from soft grass to rugged rocks, that variety naturally wears and shapes their hooves. Constant movement keeps those hooves from growing too long or becoming misshapen, a real concern for horses that lack exercise.

Now, let's talk about food. Wild horses feast on a colorful mix of grasses and plants. This balanced diet gives them the nutrients they need for healthy hooves. Just like you need vitamins for strong nails, horses need things like biotin and zinc to maintain robust hooves.

What about grooming? While wild horses don't have hoof files, they do share some tricks. They often groom each other, nibbling or picking at hard-to-reach spots. This helps keep their hooves clean and free from mud or stones that could cause problems.

Interestingly, wild horses choose their home base carefully. They prefer sandy areas, which are easier on their hooves compared to rocky terrains. That's like deciding whether to walk barefoot on a beach or on gravel. Smart move, right?

So, while they aren't savvy self-groomers in the classic sense, wild horses are the quintessential natural hoof care experts. They understand the best places to roam, they eat a healthy diet, and they team up to keep their hooves clean.

In the grand scheme of things, wild horses show us that self-care often means getting out there, moving around, and making smart choices—no fancy tools needed. So, next time you see those magnificent animals running free, remember: they're not just galloping; they're also keeping their hooftastic status with style!

11. How can you tell if a horse is happy—what signs should we look for?

When it comes to figuring out if a horse is happy, picture yourself as a playful detective on a mission to crack a fluffy mystery. Horses, those stunning creatures with flowing manes and strong legs, have a special way of showing their feelings. Their body language can tell you more than a thousand words, and luckily, you don't need a degree in horse psychology to decode their happiness.

First, let's look at their ears. Think of them as little radar dishes. If they're perked up and swiveling around, your horse is likely curious and interested. But if those ears are pinned back flat against their head, it's a clear sign that they might be feeling cranky, like a person sulking at a bad joke.

Next up is the tail. A swishing tail can tell you a lot! If it's held high and swinging playfully, your horse is feeling fantastic, as if they've just heard the best punchline. On the other hand, if the tail is clamped down, that might mean they're unhappy or uncomfortable. It's a kind of equine body language, where the tail is the emotional exclamation mark!

Now, let's check out the eyes—those windows to a horse's soul. If your horse has soft, relaxed eyes and a calm look, you can bet they're on cloud nine. Bright, wide-open eyes can mean excitement or worry, much like someone who's just drunk a double espresso.

After a nice ride or some time in the pasture, watch their behavior. A happy horse often shows playful antics, like kicking up their heels or trotting around with a spring in their step. It's as if they're saying, "Did you see how awesome that was? Let's do it again!"

And don't forget about the social side! A horse that enjoys company—whether it's you or their equine friends—is likely feeling great. If they're nuzzling their buddy or following you around, consider it a big thumbs-up for happiness.

In conclusion, while we can't directly ask horses how they feel, a little observation can go a long way. So, the next time you're near these gentle giants, keep an eye on those ears, tails, and sparkling eyes. You just might unlock the secret to equine joy. Remember, a happy horse knows how to keep its tail high and its spirits even higher—much like those of us who have just found the last slice of cake!

12. How do horses handle different climates—are they nature's ultimate survivors?

Horses, those incredible four-legged friends, truly seem like nature's ultimate survivors. Known for galloping through fields with a dancer's grace and a marathon runner's spirit, these amazing creatures have adapted to all sorts of climates and challenges over time. Let's trot through the fascinating ways horses handle different weather, shall we?

First off, let's talk about their remarkable coats. Horses can grow thicker fur in colder climates. It's like Mother Nature handed them a winter coat that puffs up all on its own! During chilly months, a horse's coat becomes long and fluffy, providing warmth. It's as if they have their own built-in heating system powered by... well, hay and oats.

In hotter climates, however, horses switch to a sleek, short coat. This change is like trading in the winter jacket for a light summer outfit. It helps them stay cool, allowing air to flow better. If only we could shed layers as easily as they do when the heat cranks up!

But it's not just about fur. Horses have an exceptional ability to regulate their body temperature. They sweat, just like us, but their sweat contains a special protein that cools them down more effectively. Ever seen a horse after a good run? Those beads of sweat glistening on their coat are not just for show; they're crucial for keeping their cool—literally!

Food and water are also major players in a horse's survival story. In tough climates where food might be hard to find, these clever creatures can thrive on rough grass. Their digestive systems are built for extracting nutrients from even the scraggliest blades. And when it comes to water, horses are smart. They instinctively know when to drink, making them experts at staying hydrated in the heat.

So, are they nature's ultimate survivors? You might think so! But let's not forget about humans. Modern domestication can complicate their survival instincts. Horses rely on their caretakers for shelter, food, and water, especially in extreme weather. So, the next time you see a horse, remember that while they have amazing adaptations, they are part of a larger team that helps them thrive.

In conclusion, horses are indeed talented survivors. With their nifty fur coats, smart temperature control, and resourceful eating habits, they show us that being able to adapt is key to life. So, whether they're leaping through snow or seeking shade on a hot day, these equines remind us that curiosity and flexibility might just be the ultimate survival skills. When life throws different climates your way, why not trot through with a bit of style?

The WHENs

No philosophers so thoroughly comprehend us as dogs and horses.

- Winston Churchill

1. When did humans start domesticating horses, and how did it happen?

The story of humans and horses is a fascinating tale that gallops through time—quite literally! It all began around 4000 to 3500 BCE in the open grasslands of Central Asia, particularly in what we now call Kazakhstan. Imagine a group of early humans, probably a bit scruffy, looking for their next meal, and stumbling upon these graceful creatures munching on grass.

At first, horses were more like big, furry lawn ornaments than trusty steeds. Early humans noticed these animals and thought, "Hmm, those could be handy." But the first step to domestication wasn't about riding. Nope! It was all about sharing meals.

People began to realize that horses could eat the same pastures their livestock were using, making them useful companions.

Let's sprinkle in a bit of science. The wild ancestors of modern horses, known as the Przewalski's horse, weren't the most cooperative. But with patience and curiosity, humans found gentler horses. This is where selective breeding made its entrance—a sort of nature's matchmaking! Imagine people picking out the friendliest horses, avoiding those that might kick or bite. They coaxed the magnificent animals with food and care. Over time, horses began to trust humans—and just like that—we went from observing to riding!

Once we cleared those initial hurdles, horses changed the game completely. They transformed transportation, trade, and even became loyal war buddies. Can you picture knights in shining armor trying to charge into battle on bicycles? Definitely not!

Fast forward a few thousand years, and horses have left their hoof prints all over human history. From the chariots of ancient civilizations to the cowboy culture in the Wild West, these majestic beasts have shaped our adventures.

In the end, the bond between humans and horses is like finding the perfect dance partner—sometimes a little awkward at first, but when you find your rhythm, you can conquer the world together. So, the next time you see a horse, who knows? You might be tempted to break out in a little dance!

2. When do horses reach full height and weight—do they have a growth spurt?

Horses and their growth patterns are a bit like watching a tall teenager trying to find their feet—awkward yet fascinating. So when do these majestic creatures reach their full height and weight? Let's trot through the basics.

Most horses are like those kids who just keep growing until they're about four to five years old. It's during this time that they experience their very own version of a growth spurt—or, as we like to call it, a "galloping growth spurt." Just like human teenagers, horses can grow a lot in a short time. Generally, you'll notice they get taller first, followed by weight.

The magic number for your average horse is around 14 to 17 hands tall (that's 56 to 68 inches for us non-horse people), depending on the breed. For example, a thoroughbred may shoot up quickly to that elegant height, while a sturdy draft horse takes a bit longer to fill out. Size can vary a lot by breed—like how some kids still fit into their old favorite jeans while others seem to burst out of their clothes overnight!

What causes all this vertical excitement? Horses' growth is ruled by their genes, nutrition, and overall health. Good food, proper care, and a little exercise help them reach their maximum potential. Think of it like giving the best fertilizer to your garden.

After five years, most horses will have reached their full height, but they still might be bulking up with muscle or shedding that last bit of puppy fat until they're around six or seven. So yes, there's a little time after the height race is over for them to fill out—like a late-night pizza run for a teenager post-growth spurt!

In conclusion, while horses don't have the "transformation montage" we see in movies, they certainly have their own natural timeline for growing tall and strong. So next time you're watching horses gallop around, just remember: they've been through their own version of awkward superhero growth phases. And who knows? Maybe one day they'll start growing taller every time we turn our backs!

3. When did horses run in the Olympics, and how has it changed over time?

Horses pranced into the Olympic Games way back in 1900—over a century ago! This was a time when folks were still figuring out what a "car" was, and horses were the stars of transportation. At the Paris Games, these equine athletes didn't just trot around. They swam and jumped too! Can you picture a horse doing the backstroke? Quite the spectacle!

Fast forward to today. Horses are still dazzling us, but the events have become a bit more refined. Now, equestrians show off their skills in dressage, show jumping, and eventing. Imagine this: one horse struts like it just won a beauty contest, another soars over hurdles as if auditioning for a superhero role, and then there's the eventing, where both horse and rider tackle a challenging course together. It's a thrilling partnership!

Here's a fun fact: humans aren't the only competitors in the Olympics. While it might seem odd for two species to team up for gold, equestrian sports showcase a unique bond. Horses and riders work together like a well-oiled machine. It's teamwork at its finest! Who knew a horse could help its rider snag a medal?

Over the years, the role of horses has transformed. In the early days, they were the main stars. Now, they share the stage with many other sports. Yet, the connection between horse and rider remains just as strong. Teamwork isn't just about sports; it's universal—even for our four-legged friends that munch on hay!

To sum it all up, from swimming horses in the early 1900s to the elegant dressage performers we see today, how we celebrate these majestic animals in the Olympics has evolved quite a bit. And while the events may have changed, one thing stays the same: we'll never look at a horse the same way again—especially if it starts doing the backstroke! Who knows what's next? Maybe a horse trying out for the gymnastics team—now that would be a sight to see!

4. When did horse racing begin, and why did it become so popular?

Horse racing, a sport that's all about thrill and showmanship, has roots that dig deep into history. Think of it as the original Formula 1, only with more hay and no pit stops. It all began around 4500 B.C. in Central Asia, where our four-legged friends first started showing off their speed. Those early races? Not quite for trophies; they were mainly about survival and migration, helping humans race through life's challenges.

Fast forward a few thousand years! By the time the ancient Greeks rolled around (about 700-500 B.C.), they realized watching horses race was much more exciting than just riding them. The Greeks included horse racing in the Olympic Games, and just like that, the stage was set for horse racing to gallop into the hearts of many. Imagine the crowds shouting, "Go, speedy horse, go!"—a fabulous scene, complete with togas instead of hotdog stands!

So why did horse racing become so popular? It's pretty simple: speed, grace, and a dose of unpredictability. Watching a horse thunder down the track can make anyone feel like a kid on a roller coaster, heart racing with excitement. And let's not forget the fun of placing a bet! It turns a laid-back afternoon into a chance to pocket some cash—a prize worth chasing!

By the Middle Ages, races were popping up all over Europe, often paired with festivals, feasting, and lively fun. The sport changed, and so did the horses. Selective breeding led to the sleek and powerful Thoroughbreds we know today. It's a mix of human skill and horse strength—a celebration of speed and strategy. Picking the right horse? That's half the thrill!

Today, horse racing still captures hearts, with famous events like the Kentucky Derby and Royal Ascot attracting crowds that rival music festivals. Whether you're there for the races or the fantastic hats, there's a little something for everyone.

So, the next time you find yourself at the racetrack, remember: You're part of an ancient tradition that's galloped through thousands of years. Where speed, strategy, and fun come together for a spectacular show. Curious about which horse will win? Just keep an eye on the fastest four legs around. Ready, set, go!

5. When did horses arrive in the Americas, and how did they impact native cultures?

Horses in the Americas? Now that's a story that trots through time! It all started when these magnificent animals were brought back by European explorers in the late 15th and early 16th centuries—around the same time Columbus was busy "discovering" the New World in 1492. Before this, horses had roamed North America eons ago, but they vanished about 10,000 years earlier. So when they returned, it was like a long-lost reunion with a fabulous twist!

Picture it: indigenous peoples spotting these sturdy, maned marvels for the first time. What a sight! Horses quickly reshaped native cultures in exciting ways. They became essential for traveling, hunting, and trading. Imagine turning a week-long walk into a breezy ride over a few days. It was like trading in your old bike for a sleek new model—much more fun and far quicker!

With the arrival of horses, the game changed. Warfare took on new dimensions. Some tribes gained major advantages in battles and expanded their territories. The horse wasn't just a way to get from point A to B; it became a symbol of status and power. Can you picture it? Riding into a meeting on a stunning stallion? Now that's what we call style!

This love affair with horses grew into something huge. The Plains tribes became well-known for their horse skills, learning to breed and train these animals like pros. They were the original cowboys, long before anyone ever wore spurs!

So here's the scoop: horses arrived in the Americas with a whinny and made a big splash, changing lives across the continent. Today, while we might think of horses as just for racing or leisurely rides, they originally sparked a cultural revolution that redefined communities.

Next time you see a horse, remember—it's not just a pretty face. It's a giant symbol of resilience, adaptation, and a legendary reunion that left lasting hoofprints on our history. So, saddle up your curiosity and dive into how these incredible creatures still enrich our world today!

6. When do horses shed their coats, and how does it help them?

Horses are amazing animals, and their seasonal coat changes are truly something to behold. So, when do these majestic creatures decide to shed their cozy fur? Generally, horses shed their coats in the spring as the weather starts to warm up. It's their version of a spring cleaning, and they take it quite seriously!

As temperatures rise and the days get longer, horses begin saying goodbye to their thick winter coats. This shedding is influenced by changes in daylight, which affects their hormones. It's like nature's gentle reminder: time to switch from that heavy winter fleece to something lighter and airier.

But why all the fuss? Shedding helps horses stay comfortable as the weather warms. That fluffy fur that kept them cozy in the cold can easily become a sauna when the sun shines. A lighter coat means better temperature control. Imagine wearing a heavy jacket in July—definitely not fun!

The benefits go beyond comfort. A fresh coat helps shed dirt, parasites, and other annoying pests. Plus, a shiny, healthy coat is a sign of a well-cared-for horse. Horse owners often beam with pride over their equine companions' glossy appearances, and for good reason!

So, the next time you see a horse rolling in the dirt and losing tufts of hair, remember: they aren't just making a mess; they're giving themselves a well-deserved makeover for the sunny days ahead. It's nature's way of helping them get ready for galloping freely under the warm sun—who wouldn't want to feel fabulous? After all, every horse knows that spring is the perfect time to show off their beautiful, sleek selves. And if that doesn't inspire you to toss off your own winter layers, what will?

7. When did the Arabian horse become famous for endurance—what's the backstory?

The Arabian horse—those graceful and spirited animals of the desert—have been famous for their endurance since ancient times. And this isn't just a recent trend; it's a story that goes back over a thousand years. To truly understand their fame, let's take a quick ride through history.

It all begins in the rugged landscapes of the Arabian Peninsula. Here, the Bedouins—nomadic tribes who moved through the desert—needed reliable companions for their long journeys. Enter the Arabian horse: small but fierce, with a heart that could outlast even the most stubborn camel. These horses weren't just pets; they were treasured family members, often sharing the tent at night!

What makes the Arabian horse so special? It's all in the genes! They have a unique body structure and a large lung capacity, making them the long-distance runners of the horse world. Think of them as the marathon champions, shaped over centuries through careful breeding. Their efficient movement allows them to save energy, making them faster when the going gets tough—like racing across the scorching desert for hours.

Now, let's fast forward to the 20th century. Suddenly, the world started to take notice. Endurance races—those thrilling long-distance challenges—showcased these incredible horses. The first organized endurance ride happened in the 1950s, where Arabian horses conquered 100 miles in a single day. Imagine that! A 100-mile sprint with legs longer than your average Tuesday commute!

As these amazing horses raced, they became celebrated not just for their speed but for their stubborn determination. From desert trails to competition tracks, Arabian horses earned their title as endurance champions, winning hearts and medals along the way.

So, the next time you see an Arabian horse moving with grace, remember: it's not just a pretty face; it's a resilient athlete. These horses carry the spirit of the desert, and when you cheer them on, you're supporting the little legend that could—because in the vast desert of life, they always find a way to win!

8. When do horses develop their distinct coat patterns—what decides the styles?

Horses and their coats are a bit like fashionistas strutting down a runway—each one showing off a look that's all their own. But when do these equine beauties decide which pattern to flaunt? Let's take a fun stroll through the world of horse genetics and a hint of nature's creativity.

First off, the secret to a horse's coat pattern is in its genes, the tiny bits that make up life. Just like a chef follows a recipe, a horse gets its coat colors and styles from its parents. These genes decide not just the color but also the patterns—spots, stripes, or that stunning splash of white known as "pinto." Different breeds can look really different; a Thoroughbred might glide by in a solid bay coat, while an Appaloosa could dazzle with spots like confetti at a party.

So, when does this coat variety make its grand entrance? Foals, those cute little bundles of joy, are born with a simple coat. As they grow, the magic begins. Around six months old, they start to show off their inherited traits—a bit like a teenager finally figuring out their style. By the time they reach two years old, they're typically fully dressed in their permanent coat patterns.

But why do they have these styles? Nature has a clever sense of fashion. Some patterns help a horse blend into their surroundings, which is super useful for dodging predators. Other styles, like the flashy spots of an Appaloosa, may help them communicate with other horses—think of it as their way of saying, "Hey, check out my unique look!"

As we trot along in the world of horse fashion, it's clear that each coat pattern tells a story—one of genes, survival, and a hint of personality. So next time you spot a horse trotting by, take a moment to enjoy its stylish coat. After all, in the horse world, every horse is a model, strutting their individual runway. And let's face it: whether they're spotted, striped, or solid, they all know how to make a grand entrance!

9. When did shire horses become essential for farming in England—are they true workhorses?

Shire horses, those gentle giants of the horse world, became essential for farming in England during the 18th and 19th centuries. They were the unsung heroes of agriculture, and it's easy to see why.

Let's take a stroll down memory lane. These powerful horses were first known in medieval times, but their size and strength made them superstars during the Industrial Revolution. As farms grew and machines started to appear, Shire horses became the go-to choice for heavy tasks—hauling plows, pulling carts full of goods, and basically being the backbone of British farming. Weighing around 1,800 pounds (that's like a small car!), they had the muscle and a calm nature, making them perfect for hard farm work—imagine a gentle giant with the strength of a heavyweight champion.

Now, here's the science behind it, but don't worry, we'll keep it simple. Shire horses are known as draft horses, which means they were bred for heavy pulling and serious work, not for speed or fancy footwork. Their large size gives them great pulling power, while sturdy legs and strong hooves help them maneuver muddy fields without sinking. Think of them as the big trucks of the horse world—built for hard work and endurance.

But what about the decline? As tractors rolled in during the 20th century, the number of Shire horses began to drop. But don't panic! These magnificent creatures are still around, cherished by many and often found in roles that showcase their beauty and strength. You might see them in parades or pulling carriages, proving they still have a lot to offer beyond the farm field.

In short, Shire horses are definitely true workhorses. They are living testaments to the hard labor that shaped England's farming success. So next time you spot a Shire horse, take a moment to appreciate the gentle giant. Behind every great farm is a story of a horse that worked tirelessly, hoof by hoof. Their legacy reminds us: sometimes, the best workers come with a little extra horsepower.

10. When did horse therapy come about—how has it changed lives?

Horse therapy, or equine-assisted therapy if you want to sound fancy, started making waves back in the 1960s. That's when people noticed something special happening: patients were lighting up and opening up while spending time with horses. Imagine finding comfort not in a traditional therapist's office, but on the back of a gentle giant. It's a bit like yoga, but with a much larger and furrier instructor.

The spark ignited when medical professionals saw how interactions with these magnificent creatures could boost well-being. It's hard to feel down while brushing a horse's mane or snuggling a soft muzzle! Fast forward to today, and horse therapy is everywhere—rehab centers, schools, community programs. It's not just for those with PTSD or physical disabilities anymore; now, people from all walks of life are seeking a dose of equine magic.

What's the science behind it? Spending time with horses has been shown to lower stress, increase confidence, and improve social skills. Caring for a horse helps you connect with your feelings, and that's no small feat. Plus, riding a horse isn't just about looking cool in a helmet. It takes balance, focus, and trust—all important parts of personal growth.

So, how has horse therapy changed lives? It's like adding a new color to your paint set. For many, it's been life-changing—helping people find themselves, manage anxiety, and build connections. Picture this: going from feeling stuck in a muddy field to galloping down a sunlit path, feeling free and alive.

In conclusion, if you ever need a boost, consider spending time with these incredible animals. They might just help you unlock a new side of yourself, all with a little help from a very large friend. Remember, where there's hoof, there's hope!

11. When did the "Renaissance of the Horse" happen, and what got invented?

The "Renaissance of the Horse" might sound like an elegant dance for horses, but it captures a lively moment from the late 20th century, especially between the 1970s and 1990s. This was when horse lovers everywhere began to deeply explore the connections between humans and their equine friends. Picture it: a joyful celebration of everything horse!

What sparked this revival? A mix of exciting factors came together. There was a growing interest in natural horsemanship, which focuses on building trust and communication between horse and rider. The days of controlling horses through fear faded away. Now, it was all about forming a partnership—think more "horse whisperer" than "horse wrestler."

During this enchanting time, several inventions galloped onto the scene, making horse enthusiasts leap for joy. For starters, we saw the rise of specialized riding gear designed not just for looks but for comfort. Imagine an ergonomic saddle that felt like sinking into your favorite armchair. Yes, that's right! Happy riders make for happy horses.

Training techniques also blossomed. Enter the round pen, a circular space that became a must-have for training. This setup allowed trainers to connect with their horses better, establishing clear communication. It wasn't just a trend; it provided a solid way to help horses build confidence and improve their skills.

Moreover, this renaissance brought about a better understanding of equine health and nutrition. Horses began enjoying meals that catered to their needs, transforming basic hay into a gourmet feast. Think of it as the "superfood revolution" for our four-legged pals, where every bite counted.

In short, while the Renaissance of the Horse didn't produce a Mona Lisa of equestrian art, it did create a major shift in how we see and relate to these incredible animals. With new training methods, comfy gear, and insights into horse care, we moved from just riding to truly partnering with them.

So next time you spot a horse strutting with pride, remember: it's living its best Renaissance life. We're just lucky to join in on the fun. After all, who wouldn't want to share life with a creature that has a flair for drama and a heart as big as a barn door?

12. When do horses grow rapidly—do they act like teenagers?

Horses do have their own version of a teenage growth spurt, and it's a sight to see! Just like human teens who suddenly need to check if their favorite sneakers still fit, young horses can grow rapidly, especially between the ages of 1 and 3.

During this time, a young horse, called a foal, can grow several inches and pack on weight. Some breeds can grow up to three inches a month during their prime growth phase! That's like a big panda trying to squeeze into its baby clothes—quite amusing!

Now, let's talk about behavior. Yes, horses can act like teenagers! Picture this: a yearling, usually around a year old, is bouncing with energy, filled with curiosity and a knack for mischief. They might gallop, nip at their buddies, and explore their place in the herd, much like a teenager testing their independence.

So, what's behind all this? Hormones are the name of the game. In horses, growth hormone and insulin-like growth factor are the big players. These hormones send signals to the body to grow, transforming a cute foal into a tall, gangly horse, sometimes looking a bit awkward—like a colt with long legs trying to figure out how to run!

And let's not forget about food! Good nutrition is key. Just like a human teen needs healthy meals to fuel their basketball dreams, horses need plenty of hay and grains to grow strong and healthy.

In the end, while horses may not share human teenage quirks, their growth spurts and lively antics certainly draw some fun parallels. So, the next time you see a young horse leaping around a field, remember: it's not just having fun; it's growing up, making friends, and navigating its own horsey social scene. Who knew that the equine teenage years could be such a captivating display?

The HUHs

The horse, the noblest creature of the earth.

- Herman Melville

1. Huh?! Did you know horses have different "whinnies" and "neighs," just like we have accents?

Horses are not just beautiful, four-legged companions; they are also vocal wizards! Just like us with our various accents, horses have their own special "whinnies" and "neighs" that can reveal a lot about where they come from and how they feel.

Studies show that a horse's sounds can change depending on its breed and surroundings. A Thoroughbred's neigh might sound quite different from an Arabian's. Think of it this way: a Londoner speaks differently than a New Yorker. This is all thanks to a mix of genes, personality, and even the influence of their owners. Isn't that fascinating?

Why does this matter? Well, those unique sounds can tell us about a horse's mood. A high-pitched whinny might suggest excitement or worry, while a low, relaxed neigh often means they're happy. So, when your horse greets you with a neigh that sounds like it's channeling a Southern belle, it might just be thrilled to see you—or maybe it's been watching too many cowboy films!

And there's more! Horses also use body language to communicate. Their ears perked up, tail swaying, and head position can add layers to what they're saying with their voices. So, if you think you can understand horse talk, remember that their body language might need its own translation guide!

Next time your horse makes a sound that catches your attention, take a moment to listen. There's a whole world of communication waiting for you to discover! You might just find that you have a knack for understanding their unique "accents." Who knows? You could become the ultimate horse whisperer among your friends!

So, whether it's in joyful whinnies or enthusiastic neighs, pay attention. Your horse has a lot to say, and those delightful sounds could lead to some fun and unforgettable conversations!

2. Huh?! Did you know horses can bolt away from danger in seconds—talk about a flight response?

Absolutely, the speed at which horses can take off is nothing short of impressive—like a furry, four-legged rocket! This awesome ability to bolt away from danger comes from their history. Picture this: horses once roamed free on the plains, dodging predators like saber-toothed cats. When faced with a threat, their instincts kick in, and it's all systems go!

Here's how it works: horses have strong muscles made for speed. Their long legs and big lungs create a perfect system for quick take-off. When a horse senses danger—like some weird rustling in the bushes—its body releases adrenaline. This hormone acts like a turbo boost. It speeds up the heart and pumps blood to those powerful leg muscles. In just a few seconds, a horse can go from casually munching grass to galloping away at speeds that can reach 40 miles per hour. That's faster than most cars in a neighborhood!

But it's not just their muscles that make horses speedy escape artists. They have top-notch senses. Horses can see nearly 360 degrees around them because of their large, side-set eyes. This means they can spot trouble coming from almost any direction. It's like having a built-in security system always on alert. Combine that with their sensitive ears, and they hear even the slightest sounds of danger.

So, the next time you see a horse take off like a champ, remember: it's not just for drama. It's a well-honed reflex that keeps them safe. They've mastered the art of survival, and that skill is super handy when those sneaky bushes start rustling!

In conclusion, horses bolt from danger not just because they can—it's in their nature. It's a mix of speed and survival, perfected over thousands of years. They look graceful as they gallop away, but really, they're experts at knowing when it's time to hoof it! So, if you ever find yourself in trouble, keep a horse nearby. They sure know how to make a swift exit!

3. Huh?! Did you know horses have been friends with humans for over 5,000 years?

It's pretty wild that horses and humans have been friends for over 5,000 years. That's a long time for two species to hang out! From brave warriors riding into battle to everyday buddies helping on the farm, horses have always trotted by our side.

So, how do we know this? Archaeologists have dug up ancient horse remains and found objects that show horses were tamed around 3500 BC in what is now Kazakhstan. Imagine it—a first selfie of a horse and rider! Initially, these majestic animals were tamed for riding and carrying heavy loads. A four-legged friend to help with work? Yes, please!

But wait! The bond didn't stop at hard work. Over time, horses became emotional companions. Picture a knight in shining armor and his gallant steed, ready to charge into danger. This partnership was about trust and loyalty. Horses can even sense our feelings! They know when we're happy or sad, making them the original therapy animals. Talk about a great listener—no judgments, just a comforting nuzzle!

With over 300 different breeds out there, you can find everything from speedy thoroughbreds to tiny ponies charming kids at petting zoos. Each breed has its own personality, just like people! Sure, a horse might not be a fan of your karaoke night, but they'd love the fresh grass you'd bring afterward.

So, next time you're chatting about amazing things, remember: horses have been part of our story for more time than many civilizations have existed. They've galloped through history with us, leaving their hoofprints in our hearts. Whether you dream of riding into the sunset or just appreciate their calm presence in a field, the horse-human friendship is a beautiful tale. It shows what happens when two species team up—sometimes for work, sometimes for fun, and always for a good story.

4. Huh?! Did you know horses can sleep standing up and lying down, depending on how safe they feel?

Horses, those amazing creatures that gallop through fields, have a quirky way of catching some sleep. They can snooze both standing up and lying down, depending on how safe they feel.

When horses catch some Z's while standing, they use a clever trick called the "stay apparatus." This system of ligaments and tendons locks their legs in place. It allows them to take a quick nap and keep alert for any lurking predators. Think of this as their all-natural security system—ideal for those moments when they need to stay one step ahead!

But when they feel safe, like in a cozy barn or surrounded by friends, they might decide to lie down and stretch out. Lying down gives them a chance for deeper sleep, including REM cycles. Yes, this means they might dream—maybe of endless pastures and a buffet of carrots! Still, they don't stay down long. Horses typically lie down for only about 30 minutes to an hour. It's all about staying cautious!

So, the next time you spot a horse dozing in the sun, remember this: it's not just napping. It's a clever dance of relaxation and alertness. These four-legged friends have mastered the art of comfort while remaining on guard. Who knew sleep could be both a science and a bit of a circus act? Being a horse is anything but simple!

5. Huh?! Did you know the Shire horse is the biggest breed, weighing up to 2,200 pounds—whoa!

The Shire horse, the gentle giant of the equine world, really knows how to stand out—especially when it tips the scales at a whopping 2,200 pounds! That's like having a small car roaming around your backyard, complete with a flowing mane and a serious appetite for hay.

Originating from England, these impressive creatures were bred for heavy farm work and hauling big loads. Their size isn't just for show; it comes from a time when they were the muscle behind farms, plowing fields and pulling carts. Talk about serious horsepower—literally! With powerful legs and sturdy bodies, they're built for strength, making them the heavyweight champs of the horse world.

Despite their size, Shire horses are known for their calm and friendly nature. Imagine a big, fluffy teddy bear, standing about 5 feet and 7 inches tall at the shoulder. You wouldn't guess that something so large could be so sweet!

And there's more! Shire horses have stunning manes and fluffy feathers around their legs, making them look like they've stepped out of a storybook. Historically, they helped with farming and even served in wars. Nowadays, you can find them at parades and festivals, proudly showing off their size and grace.

While they might not be the fastest horses around, when a Shire horse ambles by, it's hard not to smile. So next time you think of the biggest horse breed, picture a Shire trotting along—an enormous, huggable giant, who's just as curious about you as you are about it!

6. Huh?! Did you know horses can express feelings through facial expressions—watch for their "smiles"!

Horses are not just elegant animals that gallop around fields and munch on hay; they also have a unique way of showing how they feel—through their faces! Yes, you heard that right! If you've ever seen a horse, you might have caught a glimpse of what some people call a horse's "smile." But before you picture them grinning like a cartoon character, let's explore the science behind this fascinating behavior.

Horses are social creatures. Just like us, they experience a range of emotions from joy to frustration. Their faces are full of expression! When a horse is happy, you might see their ears perked up and their mouth slightly open. That's them giving you their best version of a smile! If you notice their teeth showing, that's another happy sign. But it's not all sunshine and smiles; a furrowed brow and ears pinned back can mean they're feeling upset or scared. So, if your favorite four-legged friend looks a bit grumpy, it might be time to check in on them!

In the world of horse communication, facial expressions are key. They help horses talk to each other and to us. A horse with relaxed facial muscles is usually feeling calm and happy, ready for some bonding time. On the other hand, a tense face or a wrinkled nose can signal stress. Think of it as their version of "reading the room."

This amazing ability to show feelings comes from their history. Horses are prey animals, which means they had to learn to communicate clearly to stay safe. In the wild, understanding each other can be the difference between safety and danger. So, next time you come face-to-face with a horse, really pay attention. Your equine pal might be trying to tell you they love you—or that they're just not happy with the hay selection today.

Curiosity doesn't stop at just smiles; it opens up a world where every flick of an ear and swish of a tail has a story to tell! So why not become a horse whisperer? Next time you see a horse, try to decode its facial expressions. You might discover a whole new way to understand them, one tail swish and "smile" at a time. Who knew that getting to know your horse could be so expressive—literally?

7. Huh?! Did you know the oldest horse lived to be 62 years old—what a senior!

Did you know that the longest-lived horse, a remarkable creature named Old Billy, reached the grand age of 62? That's more than just a senior; he was practically the Methuselah of the horse world! Old Billy lived in England from 1760 to 1822 and beat the average life span of horses, which is usually around 25 to 30 years. So, what made him so special?

Horses, like people, face many factors that affect how long they live, such as genetics, diet, and care. Old Billy had a steady diet of hay and a loving owner, which surely helped him reach such an impressive age. But he didn't just munch on snacks; he also worked hard, pulling barges on the River Irwell. Keeps you active, right? Maybe he knew that staying busy was the secret to a long life!

Interestingly, horses age quite differently than we do. While we might celebrate our 50s with a party, a horse in its 20s is already starting to feel its age. So, Old Billy not only defeated the odds but also showed what it means to age gracefully in the horse world.

And let's not forget the power of friendship! Horses are social creatures. Those that spend time with their buddies often stay healthier and happier. So, Old Billy probably had a lively social life, galloping with friends and sharing the latest gossip from the pasture. Who doesn't love a good chat?

In the end, Old Billy wasn't just any horse; he was a legend. His long life teaches us that it's not just about the years in your life but about the life in your years. And maybe a bit of exercise helps too! So, the next time you see a horse, give it a nod of respect. They might just have a story of longevity that rivals even the best of us!

8. Huh?! Did you know horses can recognize human faces and remember them for years?

Horses, those fascinating four-legged friends, are more than just graceful beings galloping across fields or munching on hay. They have a surprising talent: they can recognize human faces and remember them for years. Imagine them as the equine version of that friend who never forgets a face—though their friendships are forged with a sprinkle of hay and a whole lot of carrots.

Scientific studies back this up. Researchers found that horses can tell different human faces apart with impressive accuracy. In one study, horses were shown pictures of various people. They didn't just recognize familiar faces; they seemed to have favorites—just like we do at family gatherings when Aunt Edna arrives with her infamous fruitcake. These clever creatures remember the faces of people who treat them kindly, suggesting that their memories are shaped by their experiences, much like ours.

But what's behind this amazing ability? Horses are incredibly social animals. In the wild, recognizing their group mates is key to survival. This skill spills over into their interactions with us humans. They read our expressions and body language, making connections that help them navigate our sometimes confusing world.

So, when you're at the stable and your horse gives you that knowing look or seems excited to see you after a long day apart, it's not just a coincidence. They remember your face and all those adventures you've shared.

In a world filled with fleeting connections, horses remind us that relationships—whether with humans or horses—are built on recognition and understanding. Next time you stroll through a pasture, remember: you might just be in the company of some of the most perceptive "people" around, ready to forge a bond that lasts longer than your last haircut!

9. Huh?! Did you know horse races are often timed to the millisecond—no slacking allowed!

Horse racing is a sport full of excitement, steeped in tradition, where speed is everything. You heard it right—these majestic creatures are timed to the millisecond. Just imagine the pressure; even the tiniest delay could mean the difference between a shiny trophy and the disappointment of coming in second.

Let's unpack this. Timing in horse racing is super precise because every fraction of a second matters. Races use advanced electronic systems that track a horse's speed down to the tiniest tick of the clock. This accuracy is crucial for deciding the winner, setting records, and analyzing performance. It's like the Olympic sprint of the equine world, where those little milliseconds can send shockwaves through betting boards and fan hopes.

To give you some perspective, a horse galloping at about 40 miles per hour (around 64 kilometers per hour) can finish a race in a flash. If they take just a hair longer—let's say, 1/100th of a second—that could change everything. In this high-speed game, even the smallest delay can lead to a champion's glory or a runner-up's dreams dashed.

But horse racing isn't just about speed. It's a mix of strategy, breeding, and training. Just as sprinters tune their technique, trainers and jockeys work hard to get their horses in top form. Did you know some horses are specially bred for speed and stamina? It's like hitting the genetic jackpot. Certain traits can turn a horse into a champion!

So, the next time you're at a race and hear the announcer calling out those times with excitement, remember that behind each millisecond is a world of training, genetics, and maybe a sprinkle of luck.

In this thrilling world of horse racing, slow and steady doesn't win the race. Here, speed and precision are what count most. After all, in this arena, every single second matters, and a close finish is just a heartbeat away!

10. Huh?! Did you know some horses have allergies—dust, hay, or certain grasses?

Some horses can be as sensitive as that friend who can't stand the smell of your tuna salad leftovers! Just like us, horses can have allergies to things around them. Dust, hay, or even certain grasses can make them sneeze or itch. It's a surprising twist in the world of horse care!

Let's trot through the science for a moment. When a horse has an allergy, its immune system thinks a harmless thing—like dust or pollen—is dangerous. This mistaken identity leads to all sorts of annoying symptoms: coughing, runny noses, and itchy skin. Imagine feeling like you've walked into a surprise party, but instead of balloons, all you get is a cloud of dust that makes you sneeze!

Dust allergies are quite common, especially in stables that aren't cleaned regularly. Hay can be tricky too. Some hay might carry mold or other irritants that bother a horse's breathing. And then there are certain grasses that can trigger reactions—like a sudden panic attack from an unexpected encounter!

So, what do horse owners do when they discover their noble steed has allergies? They might switch to dust-free bedding, use less dusty hay, or even provide special medications—just like we take allergy pills when the pollen count rises.

In the end, horses are just like us when it comes to allergies. They may be magnificent creatures galloping through fields, but they're also sensitive beings that deserve attention when they sneeze or sniffle. Next time you see a horse, remember this: beneath that grand exterior, there could be a little drama queen battling the elements! Who knew horses could be such divas?

11. Huh?! Did you know some horses have unique skin patterns called "chrome"—nature's art?

Horses, those majestic creatures charging across fields with grace, have a fascinating trait you might not know about. Some of them display unique skin patterns called "chrome." It's like nature decided to paint a masterpiece right on their coats!

So, what is this "chrome"? In horse language, it usually refers to white markings on their fur. These can be anything from a cute star on their forehead to bold patches on their faces, legs, or bodies. It's much like how some people have trendy tattoos—each mark tells a story about their family.

What causes these quirky patterns? It's all about genetics! Yes, that mysterious code that determines who we are. Different genes control where and how big these markings are. A horse with a flashy chrome design is not just looking good; it's showing off its unique genetic mix. Kind of like how we inherit that charming smile or wild hair from our parents.

And here's a fun twist: these markings can actually serve a purpose! In the wild, a horse's pattern can help it blend into the background or stand out to potential mates. But in our modern world, it's mostly about looking fabulous. A horse with a striking chrome pattern might just grab all the attention at a local fair. Who can resist a horse with such personality?

So, the next time you see a horse rocking some stylish chrome, remember: it's not just a pretty coat but a canvas painted by genetics and nature's creativity. Here's a fun thought—if horses can wear their uniqueness with pride, why can't we? Maybe it's time for us to embrace our quirks too. After all, life is just a gallop away from being a little more colorful!

12. Huh?! Did you know horses can drink up to 10 gallons of water a day—now that's thirsty!

Horses are like the marathon runners of the animal kingdom when it comes to drinking. They can gulp down up to 10 gallons of water a day! That's quite the thirst, isn't it?

So, why do these beautiful creatures need so much H2O? It's all about their size. Horses are big—really big. An adult horse weighs anywhere from 900 to 2,200 pounds. Just like a car needs fuel to run, horses need water to keep their bodies working well. Water helps with digestion, keeps their joints moving, and supports healthy skin and coats. It's like nature's magic drink.

Let's break it down further. Horses drink more when it's warm or after a workout. They might even sip while munching hay, which can be pretty dehydrating since hay has little moisture. If a horse is sweating—like when it's racing or working hard—its need for water shoots up. Think of it as a very thirsty athlete finishing a tough training session.

But here's something fun: horses can be picky drinkers. They prefer clean, fresh water. Who wants to sip on muddy pond water? A horse's sense of taste is quite refined. They'll often turn their noses up at dirty water if they can help it. Imagine hosting a party where guests only want sparkling water—nobody likes a dirty glass!

So, the next time you see a horse lapping up water like it's at an all-you-can-drink buffet, remember it's not just about being thirsty. It's a big part of staying healthy. And while we may not drink 10 gallons ourselves, staying hydrated is just as crucial for us. After all, no one should gallop through life without their hydration.

In the end, whether it's a horse or a human, we all share one important thing: a healthy thirst for life!

Printed in Great Britain
by Amazon